REMEMBERING
GREENSBORO

REMEMBERING
GREENSBORO

JIM SCHLOSSER

THE
History
PRESS

Published by The History Press
Charleston, SC 29403
www.historypress.net

Copyright © 2009 by Jim Schlosser
All rights reserved

First published 2009

Manufactured in the United States

ISBN 978.1.59629.819.4

Library of Congress Cataloging-in-Publication Data

Schlosser, Jim.
Remembering Greensboro / Jim Schlosser.
p. cm.
ISBN 978-1-59629-819-4
1. Greensboro (N.C.)--History--Anecdotes. 2. Greensboro (N.C.)--Biography--
Anecdotes. 3. Greensboro (N.C.)--Social life and customs--Anecdotes. 4. Guilford
County (N.C.)--History, Local--Anecdotes. I. Title.
F264.G8S35 2009
975.6'62--dc22
2009042618

Dedicated to my wife of more than four decades, whom I call Cathy, but who prefers Kate.

CONTENTS

CONTENTS

ACKNOWLEDGEMENTS

I am grateful for so many who helped with this book, some of whom don't know that they did. I'm talking about editors through the years who edited these stories and made them better. They removed what came to be known at the *Greensboro News & Record* as "Schlosserisms." This is my tendency to write "plaque" when I mean "plague" or "trial" when I mean "trail."

The book also couldn't have been done without the help of Diane Lamb, librarian at the *News & Record*, who searched for old stories and photos and let me poke through the library's files. I also want to thank Stephen Catlett, the curator of the vast treasure of photos at the Greensboro Historical Museum.

I've been using computers for years but still don't understand them. I'm grateful to Libby Stafford for her help in showing me how to organize electronically the book from the title page to the last story. Thanks also go to Gayle Fripp, an esteemed local historian who edited my first book, *The Beat Goes On…*, a collection of stories. She kept meticulous files and turned over a box of more than 1,500 stories she had read for *The Beat Goes On…*

HAPPENINGS

A RETURN TO WHERE
HISTORY WAS MADE

The test of Josephine Boyd Bradley's feelings about Grimsley High School, where students taunted and threw slurs and rubbish at her forty-eight years ago, came at the end of the ceremony. Could she bring herself to sing the alma mater with the audience?

She did so with gusto from the stage of the school, which honored her on Friday as the first black student at the school and, in 1958, the first black to graduate. She also was the first black person to graduate from a previously segregated school in North Carolina.

Irony was obvious in the auditorium. The school that shunned her in 1957 and 1958 was giving her the hero's treatment. Principal Rob Gasparello said that Grimsley—now 30 percent black—was "celebrating part of the past we don't like to look at but from which we can learn."

Speakers recounted the eggs tossed, racial slurs shouted and thumbtacks placed on her chairs. Bradley was so afraid of the cafeteria that she initially ate in the library.

No apology was given Friday, although City Councilwoman Diane Bellamy-Small, who presented Bradley the key to the city and sang "Lift Every Voice and Sing," also known as the "Black National Anthem," said that all black people are owed one. The word "thanks" was spoken instead. "Thank you for the great personal sacrifice for such an important cause," said school historian Peter Byrd, class of '74.

Applause swept the auditorium when Byrd, who is white, said, "I'm very proud that I got to graduate from your high school." He kissed her.

Civil rights pioneer Josephine Boyd Bradley, first black student at Grimsley High School, visits school in 2006 as a professor at Clark Atlanta. *Courtesy of* Greensboro News & Record.

Julia Adams, one of three white students who, back then, invited Bradley to eat with them in the cafeteria, called Bradley one of the most courageous people she ever met. She said she changed the city forever, for the better.

Wearing a vest that said "Greensboro Senior High 1958," college professor Bradley, who lives in Atlanta, rose several times to accept mementos. Each time, a smartly attired student, Bane Sanaland, hurried forward to take her arm. Bradley laughed appreciatively. She chuckled about the limousine ride to campus.

Bradley said she had refused to cry during that long-ago year, "but now I know I can let the tears flow." "I know the mission has been accomplished," she said.

An outstanding student at then all-black Dudley High, she was persuaded to transfer to what was then called Greensboro Senior High—1 black student among 1,950 whites. "Talk about minority," she said. Civil rights leaders had wanted to test the city's willingness to integrate.

She read a letter that her late father, who was illiterate, dictated shortly before she enrolled. He knew that abuse was ahead and told her, "Find a place in your heart to go when things get rough, be free of anger and hate" and "remember you are there because you have a right to be."

As for recent stories about the school apologizing, she said, "There is no need for anyone to apologize or say I'm sorry." The ceremony speaks for itself, she said.

Her portrait, by Winston-Salem artist Leo Rucker, was unveiled and will hang in the main hall with a plaque. The plaque's frame comes from the old library, where, as one speaker put it, Bradley sought refuge "as a humble hero" who "grew up in a difficult time."

Originally published in 2006.

THE BEWILDERING CASE
OF FRITZ KLENNER AND SUSIE LYNCH

About 3:10 p.m. on June 3, 1985, Kerry Loggins, a thirteen-year-old Northwest Junior High School student, stepped off the school bus at NC 150 and Strader Road in Summerfield. Loggins was met by Benji, his dog, who started barking at the sound of approaching sirens from the west on NC 150.

"You could hear the noise of a four-wheel-drive vehicle and those big tires moving," he said.

He chased after Benji, running toward the sirens. "All of a sudden I saw the explosion," Loggins said. "It looked like black dust, like tar flying. I turned around because I didn't want to see what it was like after the dust settled."

The scene was one of the most gruesome ever in Guilford County. Debris covered the highway for a long stretch. What was left of the chassis of a Chevy Blazer was next to a horse pasture.

On one side of the highway, in a roadside ditch, lay the bodies of two adults thrown from the exploding car. Two dead children and two dead dogs remained inside what was left of the Blazer.

Sheriff deputies, state troopers and other law enforcement officers who had been chasing the Blazer told people rushing out of homes and cars to view the carnage to stay back. The officers warned that another explosion was possible.

What happened that day on the rural highway ended a series of murders that had taken place in Winston-Salem, Greensboro, rural Guilford County and Louisville, Kentucky. Never before had local officers confronted such a perplexing case that wiped out two prominent families related by marriage, and whose members included Susie Sharp, chief justice of the North Carolina Supreme Court.

The killers were Frederick "Fritz" Klenner, thirty-two, of Reidsville and his first cousin and lover, Susie Newsom Lynch, who was a graduate student at the University of North Carolina at Greensboro and lived in an apartment with her two children, John, age ten, and Jim, age nine, and Fritz Klenner.

Besides blowing themselves up in the Blazer that Fritz Klenner had bomb rigged, he and Susie Lynch, evidence would later show, had also poisoned and killed her two sons by a marriage that had ended a few years before.

Klenner, with a passion for firearms, knives and explosives, had earlier in the year killed his and Susie Lynch's grandmother, Hattie Newsom, and Susie's parents (Fritz's aunt and uncle), Robert and Florence Newsom of Greensboro, at Hattie's Winston-Salem home. Months earlier, Klenner had shot and killed Susie Lynch's former mother-in-law, Delores Lynch, and former sister-in-law, Janie Lynch, both of Louisville, Kentucky. Police later came to believe that Susie Newsom Lynch was Fritz's accomplice in all the murders.

The explosion that finally ended the killing spree came twenty-five minutes and fifteen miles after police tried to arrest Klenner at the busy intersection of West Friendly Avenue and College Road, in front of the entrance to the Guilford College, a school founded in 1837 by Quakers and dedicated to peace.

A woman was pumping gas at a Wilco station across from the college. A stray bullet singed through her car's open door and exited out the windshield. Unknown to her, carloads of officers were trying to arrest Fritz Klenner, who was escaping with Susie Lynch, her sons (believed to be alive at the time) and their dogs. The police had warrants charging Klenner with murder. In his hometown of Reidsville, Klenner had fooled people, including his father, who was a doctor, into thinking that he was a physician. He worked with his father and treated patients.

Klenner lived in Greensboro in an apartment with Susie Lynch and her two children by her marriage to former Wake Forest University basketball player Tom Lynch, then a dentist in New Mexico.

Klenner fired on the officers, wounding Greensboro officer Tommy Dennis in the chest and winging two Kentucky cops. The Kentuckians were there to interrogate Klenner about the deaths of Susie Lynch's mother-in-law and sister-in-law.

Fritz Klenner, armed with an Uzi machine gun and other weapons, fired wildly. A man in the left-turn lane of Friendly, waiting to turn onto College

Road, saw his windshield explode. He thought at first that a car wreck had occurred next to him but then noticed that his own windshield was gone.

Kathy Galloway of Greensboro and Bernie Greeson, visiting from Denver, were driving west on Friendly when the Blazer pulled beside them. Galloway said that police were behind the Blazer when the driver got out and began firing. She remembers him using two weapons. "We just ducked," Galloway says.

Tellers at a Wachovia Bank branch on one side of the intersection heard gunshots, looked out the window and saw a man, Klenner, shooting. The tellers locked the bank's door."

Klenner jumped back into his SUV and banged into several cars with his Blazer's special steel bumper to push them from his escape path. He took off down New Garden Road, which starts on the other side of the intersection, where College Road ends.

A caravan of officers pursued, staying at a distance because Klenner stopped periodically and fired shots. An airplane overhead radioed cops when Klenner was stopping.

At the intersection of NC 150 and U.S. 220 in Summerfield, two sheriff's deputies hoped to intersect Klenner. He blew right by them. Sheriff Jim Proffit said that Klenner looked at the deputies, David Thacker and Herbert Jackson, "and smiled at them."

Deputies Thacker and Jackson joined the other officers pursuing Klenner. Thacker and Jackson got the closest to the Blazer, but they could only see a flurry of movement inside. NC 150 rounded a bend and became a straightaway just past where Bronco Lane intersected.

Beside Sunburst horse farm, the deputies saw a gun barrel emerge from the Blazer's window. At that moment, the explosion occurred, killing all inside. According to *Bitter Blood*, a bestselling book about the Klenner murder spree by Jerry Bledsoe—a former *News & Record* writer—the bomb was planted under Susie Lynch's seat. Police believe that Susie Lynch gave her consent to planting the bomb and may have detonated it.

The motive for all this killing: child custody. Tom Lynch was seeking custody of the boys after becoming distressed at his former wife's and Wake Forest classmate's behavior. Dr. Lynch thought that Susie's relationship with her cousin was unseemly and set a poor example for the boys. Fritz's aunt and uncle, Robert and Florence Newsom, felt the same way. So did his grandmother, Hattie Newsom. Along with Dr. Lynch's mother and sister, they were supporting the dentist in his bid to gain custody of the boys.

Police believe that Kenner wanted to kill all in the custody case, including Dr. Lynch, who probably would have been the next target. He and Susie were determined to keep the children.

Clyde Robinson Jr. was standing in his yard trying to sell a car to a man when he saw and heard the "unreal" blast. His wife, Pauline, said that it shook the foundations of the house. "We've been in the pits at the Daytona raceway when all the cars were in there making noise," Pauline said, "and it was comparable to what happened here."

Until after dark that Monday, crowds gathered at the roped-off site. Firetrucks and ambulances lined the road where the blast occurred. Two vehicles from a company that removes bodies from crime scenes waited for officers to finish with their work before moving in. White sheets covered the bodies of Klenner and Lynch. A Greensboro firetruck arrived with a cherry picker so officers could take elevated pictures of the debris.

There was no doubt, as police later studied the case, that Klenner and Lynch had committed suicide after earlier killing young John and Jim. The police also believe that Fritz Klenner was trying to escape to a hideaway in his native Rockingham County where he kept weapons and tried out explosives.

Back at the explosion scene on NC 150, the crowd had to run for cover when a horrific hailstorm started dropping marble-size stones on the landscape. Bledsoe, in *Bitter Blood*, quotes Kentucky detective Lieutenant Dan Davidson as saying, "It was like the Lord was mad. Like He was real mad. I mean really pissed off."

Originally published in 1985.

Author's note: After Jerry Bledsoe's book came out, Hollywood snapped up the story. *Bitter Blood* later became a major motion picture starring Kelly McGillis as Susie, Harry Hamlin as Fritz Klenner and Keith Carradine as Tom Lynch.

THE HARDY BOYS TAKE ON
OPPOSING ROLES AT TANK FARM STRIKE

For Rickey and Lonnie Hardy, it's brother against brother. Each morning, they stand at their separate posts at petroleum storage tanks near the Greensboro airport. It is the scene of a massive strike by independent truckers enraged about ever-increasing fuel costs. The governor has mobilized the National Guard to keep peace.

Rickey Hardy wears green fatigues with chevrons on the collar and a steel helmet with a protective shield over the face. He carries an M-16 rifle. His cartridge belt includes several magazines of live ammunition. He's there to make sure that striking drivers don't disrupt those who continue to make deliveries and pick up fuel loads at the enormous petroleum complex known as the "tank farm."

Bluntly, Rickey Hardy is there to guard against the likes of his brother, Lonnie Hardy.

Lonnie pickets about a block away. He's older and slightly heavier than Rickey. He wears a Western hat, a soiled shirt and jeans. He needs a shave. His face is sunburned from long days at the tank farm. He's been spending nights sleeping with his wife in his rig parked off old U.S. 421, which passes the farm. He walks up and down the highway with a sandwich board draped around his neck, a message to passing motorists: "Going broke, shutdown… Need relief."

Normally colorful and talkative, Lonnie Hardy clams up on the subject of his brother. "I figure family matters are personal. I'll just say there will be no conflict between me and my brother over this. We'll get along again afterward," said Lonnie, an army veteran who served in Vietnam and now lives in his rig year-round.

Rickey, who works in civilian life for a transmission company in Winston-Salem, is more talkative. "I sympathize with Lonnie's cause," he says. "I understand what he is doing. I just hope he understands what I am doing and why I have to do it."

The night Governor Jim Hunt activated four hundred guardsmen for duty in Greensboro, Rickey saw Lonnie, who said, "'I'll be out there with you.' And here we are." Rickey learned that he had been called to duty while fishing at a placid lake along the same highway, 421. He was daydreaming about a coastal trip this weekend with his father-in-law.

"My wife came running up to tell me what she had just heard on the television," Rickey says. "I thought she was kidding at first. Finally, I went home, packed and went to the armory. I guess I won't be going to the coast this weekend."

Originally published in 1979.

Author's note: The strike caused many exchanges of angry words between strikers and nonstrikers but ended without violence, with the Hardy boys going back to their civilian routines.

SLEEPY BRAKEMAN RESPONSIBLE FOR ONE OF COUNTY'S WORST TRAIN WRECKS

Maybe the term "asleep at the switch" arose from this accident. On the night of October 17, 1907, southbound freight train No. 83 entered a siding near Rudd Station, a former rural Guilford County depot next to the present entrance to the Bryan Park soccer complex off Lee's Chapel Road.

No. 83 made the move to allow Washington-bound passenger train No. 34 to pass on the main tracks. No. 83's brakeman, H.C. Leonard, locked the siding switch to prevent No. 34 from entering the siding and hitting Leonard's train.

Leonard was bone tired. He and his crew had been working for twenty-three hours. After actually locking the switch, he sat down and fell asleep. When he awoke, he heard No. 34 approaching. Dazed, he forgot that he had locked the siding switch. He unlocked it, thinking that he was locking it.

No. 34 roared into the siding and into No. 83. Five people died and twenty others were injured; many were sent to St. Leo's Hospital in Greensboro. The accident was eerily similar to another involving No. 34 the previous year, when an open switch in Greensboro's Pomona freight yard had sent the passenger train smashing into another train, killing four crew members.

After the accident at Rudd Station, H.C. Leonard panicked and fled. He walked through the woods for three days without food to reach his home in the railroad town of Spencer, sixty miles away. In late October, he returned to Guilford County and was arrested at the train station. Instead of jailing Leonard, the deputy guarded him that night at the Clegg Hotel next to the

Site of the deadly 1907 train wreck at Rudd Station caused by a drowsy brakeman who failed to lock a switch. *Photo by Jim Schlosser.*

station. The following day, a coroner's jury, similar to a grand jury, indicted Leonard for manslaughter. His mother arrived and posted a $1,000 bond.

The accident came in an era when train wrecks seemed almost as common as auto crashes today. In addition to the deadly accident at Pomona the year before, another that year, in southern Virginia, killed Southern Railway's president, Samuel Spencer, the namesake of Leonard's hometown. Spencer had just finished a hunting trip in Guilford County and was headed back to Southern's headquarters in Washington when another train rear-ended his.

As the saying goes, justice delayed is justice denied. When H.C. Leonard's case came up in the December 1907 term of Guilford's Superior Court, it was continued without explanation. During the January 1908 term, it was continued again, with no reason given. In April 1908, another continuance was granted, the reason given that "a material witness" was not available. After that, Leonard's case wasn't mentioned in the press when court convened for the rest of 1908 and well into 1909. Court records for that period are not available. Perhaps the case was settled between court sessions.

By 1910, Leonard apparently no longer lived in Spencer. A Salisbury-Spencer city directory contains no listing for him.

That accident and others motivated Southern Railway. It had earlier begun—but stopped because of a national economic downturn—to double

Norfolk Southern locomotives approaching the Rudd Station Road crossing, where the depot and siding were in 1907. *Photo by Jim Schlosser.*

track its Washington–Atlanta mainline. This would allow north- and south-bound trains to pass without pulling into sidings. Double tracks could have prevented the 1907 accident.

Double tracking resumed in 1909 and was eventually completed. Sections of double track were ripped up in the 1970s as a cost saver. By then, Southern had a centralized traffic control system designed to keep trains apart. Long before that, it began reforms about how long a crew could stay on duty.

The road into Bryan Park crosses the tracks at the intersection of Rudd and Lee's Chapel Roads. The siding where No. 34 and Freight No. 83 met more than 101 years ago is long gone.

Originally published in 2009.

TWO SURVIVORS OF
THE 1948 POLIO EPIDEMIC

Clara Sineath and Royce Barham are two children of 1948, the year Guilford County suffered through one of the worst polio epidemics in the United States. Both were stricken that summer, when the epidemic raged at its worst. Playgrounds, swimming pools and theatres closed. Parents sent children to grandparents in the country. One mom tied her five-year-old to the porch to keep him from wandering to a neighbor's yard and catching the potentially crippling disease.

It is a stretch to call Sineath a child of '48. She was twenty-four then, proof that polio didn't attack just children, though most victims were. She awoke one morning feeling headachy and feverish, "as though I was coming down with the flu," she says.

She was certain that her feeling ill was related to her being nine months pregnant. She telephoned her obstetrician, who told her to rest and call back if she felt worse. Later that day, her neck stiffened. She became terrified. Neck stiffness was often an early sign of polio. Newspapers had repeatedly reported stories about early symptoms. She summoned her doctor, who, after examining her, left and returned with another physician. Together, they agreed that it was polio.

Sineath was rushed to a temporary, heavily quarantined polio hospital in a lofty, tar-papered structure that a few years before had been a recreation hall for a temporary World War II Army Air Corps base. It was built in a matter of months in 1943 and eventually housed forty thousand troops.

"They must have given me some kind of drug that night because the next thing I remember was awakening the next morning and being shown a healthy, seven-pound baby boy," Sineath says. "I was so happy when I saw that baby [her first] that I tried to reach out to it, but I found I couldn't move. I suddenly remembered I had polio."

Fortunately, Sineath's case turned out to be mild and nonparalytic, although she was on her back for three months. She was allowed to see her baby for five minutes a day. It was against hospital rules for patients to see spouses, but her husband, L.C. Sineath, got a job moonlighting as a hospital volunteer, administrating hot packs to infant polio patients.

Clara Sineath, who lived in northeast Greensboro at the time, knows that she was one of the lucky ones. She recalls another patient who arrived the same night she did, also an adult. "I remember his wife saying she was going to the car to get him a radio. He told her, 'Don't bother because I am not going to make it, I'm going to die.' And he did. That night."

The child born to her at the polio hospital, Bythel, grew up, served in Vietnam, graduated from Appalachian State University and married.

Royce Barham was only two years old in 1948 and remembers nothing about being stricken except what his mother told him later. "She had finished working the fields one day and went to pick me up but couldn't get me to stand," he says. "I kept falling down. She thought nothing of it at first, but later, when I still couldn't stand, she called the doctor."

Barham was paralyzed. His first recollection of life is being one of the youngsters in diapers on the long rows of beds in the old army base building. It was the start of a long ordeal with the aftereffects of polio. He wore leg braces and used crutches until he was nine. Before he was twelve, he had undergone four polio-related operations. "The doctor wanted me to have a fifth operation, but I just told him, no, I couldn't stand any more hospitals or pain," says Barham, who during this long recovery period once spent thirteen months at Winston-Salem's Baptist Hospital after surgery.

In his teens, he was determined to be an athlete. He lifted weights and did other exercises and saw improvement. He played sandlot football. "I don't believe there was another kid who loved sports more than I did, and heck yeah I got out there and tried some football," he says. "But I soon discovered my best effort was not as good as the worst effort of another boy with two good legs."

He's not bitter today. He likes his job (he is a fast-food outlet manager) and is grateful that his own two children didn't have to fear the coming of summer and polio season. The Salk and Sabin vaccines of the early 1950s virtually wiped out polio. "I think it's great they can look forward to summertime," he says. "Everyone dreaded it when I was a young kid."

Originally published in 1975.

TWO JACKSONS, ONE WHITE, ONE BLACK, ONCE FOES, STAND TOGETHER

Two Jacksons stood side by side in Greensboro on Wednesday, as they had twenty years ago. This time, one of them hoped that he was headed to the White House rather than the Guilford County Jail.

Presidential candidate Jesse Jackson publicly embraced and joked with his foe from the segregated past, retired Greensboro police detective William Jackson. Detective Jackson on several occasions arrested civil rights demonstrator Jesse Jackson in the early 1960s.

The younger Jackson was then the student body president at North Carolina A&T State University and is now an internationally known figure for his political and civil rights work.

As the black candidate and white officer stood together on a platform in the chilly air outside A&T's administration building, three to four hundred students watched. The retired detective beamed as Jesse Jackson called the officer "a very special person" and praised him for doing his job fairly and nonviolently during that turbulent period of social change in the South.

"No dogs bit anyone here," Jesse Jackson said of the mass downtown desegregation protests he led in 1963 in downtown Greensboro. "No one was murdered here or beaten here," he said.

The demonstrations came three years after the now famous Greensboro sit-ins, when four A&T students sat down at the whites-only Woolworth's lunch counter on South Elm Street and refused to leave after being denied service. That began daily sit-ins that lasted on and off for six months. It finally ended with the integration of Woolworth's and nearby Kress dime

Jesse Jackson leaving jail after his arrest for blocking traffic during a demonstration against segregation in downtown Greensboro. *Courtesy of* Greensboro News & Record.

store, but left the rest of downtown still segregated. The Jesse Jackson–led marches resulted in the desegregation of all of downtown.

So many students participated and were arrested—including for blocking the city's main downtown intersection—that an empty, former polio hospital had to be turned into a temporary jail. The actions of the Greensboro police were "in great contrast to Birmingham," Jesse Jackson

The two Jacksons—Jesse (left) and Bill—in the late 1970s, no longer adversaries as in 1963. *Courtesy of* Greensboro News & Record.

said, referring to the Alabama city where violent reaction by police against protesting black students is considered one of the low points in the nation's civil rights movement.

Chuckling, Jesse Jackson said that the officer arrested him by saying, "I'm glad to see you. Take those handcuffs and put them on." He added, "He did his job, but understood our job at the same time."

The crowd, which included about fifty reporters from all over the nation, roared when Jesse Jackson turned to William Jackson and said, "If I'm elected I will name him a U.S. marshal." He described the other Jackson as representative of the change and transition that results "if people have a common agenda."

Detective Jackson didn't address the crowd but later told reporters that Jesse Jackson as a student "was a nice fellow who knew where he was headed." Asked if he would vote for Jackson, William Jackson replied, "I will vote the dictates of my heart."

Where are those?

"I don't know," he said.

Originally published in 1984.

PLACES

GUILFORD'S LAST OLD-TIME ROADHOUSE NO LONGER AN ISOLATED PLACE ON HIGHWAY

Whitsett—The future doesn't look bright for the Brightwood Inn, the closest thing to a genuine roadhouse in Guilford County. Since 1936, when it began as a truck stop, the Brightwood has stood isolated along a stretch of U.S. 70 beside a horse pasture between Burlington and Greensboro. The restaurant and bar survived the opening in the mid-1950s of Interstate 85, which took traffic off Highway 70. More recently, the Brightwood has bucked competition from chain bars and grills with Irish names that have multiplied in Burlington and Greensboro. Business remains good, says owner Paul Treadway, though not as good as in the 1950s. Back then, people lined up, even paid a cover charge, to get inside for dining and dancing.

Two threats now make regular customers worry about what's around the bend for the landmark: the advancing ages of Treadway, seventy-four, and his longtime, loyal staff; and creeping suburbanization.

The Brightwood soon will have company—a lot of company. What amounts to a new city will arise on a 512-acre horse farm behind the inn. Westminster Homes of Greensboro plans 2,500 homes, town houses and businesses there. Randy Sexton, a Westminster executive, says that the company has no interest in the 4-acre slice that the Brightwood Inn occupies.

Don't believe it, Treadway says. "They would love to have it," he says from behind the counter of the short-order part of the business. "I'll never sell." The green counter with green stools occupies the narrow, knotty-pine paneled center of the building. A long, paneled barroom is on the left; two dining rooms with tables and booths are on the right.

Brightwood Inn, part of the small town of Whitsett, has withstood the encroachment of subdivisions. *Photo by Jim Schlosser.*

In one of those booths, Elvis Presley ate a hamburger with tomato and lettuce and downed a pint of milk while a female companion sipped a Miller High Life. Presley wasn't famous then. It wasn't until later that the woman, who lived in Burlington, called the inn to say that the king of rock 'n' roll had dined at the Brightwood.

Behind the green counter hang thousands of hats that customers and strangers bring to Treadway, as well as cigar boxes, unusual soda bottles and other knickknacks. Treadway's a pack rat. A Chrysler of 1940s vintage looks abandoned in the parking lot. Treadway says that it's road worthy, if the tires had air. He keeps a procession of cars dating back decades. "I buy one, drive it for ten years, park it, buy another, drive it for ten years, park it and..." he says.

While he enjoys the past, he's not stuck in it. He says that he welcomes the coming of Brightwood Farm, although he wishes long-ago plans for two golf courses on the horse farm had been carried out. He says the new development will help the Whitsett/Gibsonville area. Besides, when Brightwood Farm is fully developed, he doubts he'll be there to see what impact it will have on the inn. Treadway is assisted by Lucille Little, seventy-one, who has worked there forty-nine years; his sister/cook, Carolyn Sutton, sixty-six; and dishwasher Edward Kerr, sixty-two. "I can't be here much longer," he says. "Lucille can't be here much longer."

The Brightwood Inn. *Photo by Jim Schlosser.*

A bachelor, he has no children waiting to take over. When he departs, he says, the decision of whether to stay open will be Little's. She shakes her head at the thought of Treadway—the chatterbox—not being around to greet customers. "It wouldn't be the same without him," Little says.

The inn's lonely, lovely setting beside an old highway and its dark, paneled interior add charm and mystique. The Brightwood could have served as the roadhouse setting in James M. Cain's novel, *The Postman Always Rings Twice*. A family had started the Brightwood in 1936 to cater to truckers on U.S. 70, then the main east–west highway through the state. An Elon College (now university) professor later bought the place and turned it into a diner and restaurant. Treadway bought it in 1950. He added a second dining room and a barroom and called the place an inn—though it has no rooms for rent. He says "inn" sounds more family-friendly than "bar" or "tavern."

Treadway says that he's never had a lick of trouble at the Brightwood. He describes his customers as classy people from all over the area.

The inn has cut back offerings. Dancing and curb service were dropped years ago, though hundreds of rusty bottle caps remain in the parking lot as a reminder of hustling carhops. Lunch is no longer served.

Treadway could afford to retire. He owns plenty of real estate and won $1.25 million in the Virginia lottery in 1992. But he enjoys being at the Brightwood, with its clientele that represents two and three generations.

Dawn Thornburg studied the songs on the jukebox in the bar and said that her mother and grandmother had been regulars at the Brightwood. The three used to ride horses to the inn, hitching them to the fence next to the parking lot. "I remember the first time I came when I was about seven. We ate pizza," says Thornburg, thirty-three.

Treadway repeats that old age—his and that of his staff—will be what dooms the Brightwood Inn in the end. Life is like the highway outside. "How far down the road can you go?" he asks.

Originally published in 2002.

Author's note: The Brightwood continues, with houses creeping closer.

MINING LONG GONE
BUT AN OLD ENGINE HOUSE HAS NEW PURPOSE AND SERVES AS REMINDER OF GUILFORD'S GOLD-DIGGING DAYS

Jamestown—Unlike most ghost towns, Gardner Hill left no trace—not a saloon, a church, a store or houses. An estimated five hundred people appeared to have vanished before 1850 without leaving a trace, other than boarded-up gold mines.

Gardner Hill stood in southwest Guilford County on Wiley Davis Road, in what is now the Sedgefield golfing community, where each August golf pros mine for more than $5 million in prize money in what's now the Wyndham Championship PGA Tour tournament.

Gardner Hill residents dug for gold, and found it for a time. The community may have been a common town for all miners who worked in Gardner Hill and at other nearby mines—Fisher, Deep River Hill, Fentress, North State (later renamed McCullough Mine), Hodges—in southwest and western Guilford. These mines were part of what geologists call the Carolina Igneous Belt, extending from here west to Mecklenburg County, where near Charlotte is the Reed Gold Mine, a state historic site.

Geologists say that the miners left behind plenty of gold, although it is difficult to tap. No one has come forth during the recent hard times to try, even though the price of gold reached an all-time high.

Gardner Hill's population in the 1840s would have made it the county's largest town. Greensboro, founded in 1808, consisted of only a few hundred residents. High Point didn't even exist. It would be founded in 1856, the highest point on the new North Carolina Railroad.

The remains of the shaft from Gardner Hill Gold Mine near Jamestown. *Courtesy of* Greensboro News & Record.

The engine house at the old McCullough Mine before restoration. *Courtesy of* Greensboro News & Record.

It is probably safe to assume that these mining villages were rowdy, with brothels, gambling and other sins.

Many of the miners came from Wales, says county historian James G. MacLamroc. In addition to the Welshmen, the mines were known to use plenty of black slaves, probably assigned to the most dangerous tasks beneath the earth.

At Gardner Hill, the mine overlooked a stream. Near the stream in the early 1970s were the remains of moonlike craters about six to eight feet deep. Roger Sharpe, a UNCG student who was researching the mines, said that miners dug the craters looking for gold close to the surfaces.

Gardner Hill had five main shafts, the deepest about 268 feet straight down. The vertical mines were said to have had levels where miners could veer off and work tunnels that formed right angles to the main shaft. Some of these side shafts extended 500 feet.

Documents on file in Raleigh indicate that Gardner Hill produced $100,000 worth of gold, probably during the 1840s to early 1850s. This figure may be conservative. Some gold may have gone unreported to bypass the taxmen. After the California gold rush began, Gardner Hill's operation continued until the Civil War, when the shafts were shut down. In the 1930s, Greensboro cotton broker James Latham, who gave land for what's now Latham Park in Greensboro, drained water from the shafts, with the idea of resuming mining during the Depression. Gold would have been far more valuable than currency. But Latham never followed through. Later, the mining shafts at Gardner Hill and at several other mines were filled in for safety reasons.

The closing of the shafts didn't discourage some prospectors. Reuben Allred of Jamestown, who lived near the mines, kept panning streams for

A modern photograph of the restored rock engine house at McCullough Mine. *Photo by Jim Schlosser.*

Castle McCullough, the former rock engine house, is now used for social events. *Photo by Jim Schlosser.*

gold until the 1970s. His perseverance, he once said, helped him to weather the Depression.

Several mines lingered on until the 1900s, including the Deep River Mine. Another North State mine survived until the 1880s. Its remains were visible in the 1970s in the woods off Business Interstate 85 near Jamestown.

The most eye-catching structure was the mine's rock house, or engine room, where a steam engine ran the mining equipment. The exhaust left by way of a 160-foot chimney. The still standing chimney includes a ghost story of a young girl plunging to her death. The reddish substance on the rocks in the stream below is said to be her blood. Workers entered the room through an arched door on which "1833" was barely legible. One of North State's shafts was 353 feet deep. Before it closed, the mine extracted more than $126,000 in gold and copper.

The engine room has been restored and the area around it landscaped. It's now called Castle McCullough, a privately owned place popular for weddings, parties and other social events.

While California and Alaska are considered America's gold states, few people realize that North Carolina was the nation's leading gold-producing state up to 1850. Miners at the Reed Mine uncovered a nugget weighting twenty-eight pounds.

Originally published in 1973.

WHAT LOOKS SO ORDINARY NOW, BLACKS AND WHITES AT A DIME STORE LUNCH COUNTER, WAS CONSIDERED UNTHINKABLE TWO DECADES AGO

It only takes about two sips of cup at the Woolworth's lunch counter before the absurdity of twenty years ago becomes apparent. "Sure, when you look back, I guess it does look silly," says Woolworth's manager Andy Moye. "It's hard to explain to young people today just how it was. They can't visualize or understand why it was the way it was."

Moye, who has worked for the dime store chain for forty-four years, is seated at the counter smoking a cigarette, surveying the crowd of customers coming in and out of entrances along South Elm Street and Sycamore Street.

White and black waitresses stay busy with orders and delivering blue-plate specials, snatching away empty plates. A black woman cooks behind the counter. Another rings up the cash register.

Black and white customers sit along the winding counter eating, drinking and talking. The scene looks so natural and common, yet one like it caused an uproar on February 1, 1960, an event that focused international attention on Greensboro.

The Greensboro sit-ins took place when four black North Carolina A&T State University students came into the store, sat down at the whites-only counter, asked for service and were refused. They stayed seated until the then manager, Curley Harris, shut down the store early.

The sit-ins have been declared a watershed event in the nation's civil rights movement. Other sit-ins had been attempted, but none was successful. The original four students, later joined by hundreds of others, black and white, returned off and on for six months. Integration finally came, and Greensboro inspired black students to stage lunch counter sit-ins throughout the South.

Paul Leacraft, a young black girl, enjoys her meal, with a white person seated on her right. "I was three years old when it happened," she says. "I don't remember segregation. My brother and parents used to tell me about it. I have been doing some thinking, trying to imagine what it must have been like."

Nearby, James Brandon, a young black man, slides into a seat and orders a milkshake. A white waitress brings it and requests that he take a swallow to make sure it is as he wants it. "I was only about six years old when the sit-ins occurred," Brandon says. "I guess it was pretty rough for blacks back in those days."

Brandon says that he has never experienced discrimination, except for an occasional glare or ugly word directed at him when he enters a place that is predominantly white. How would he have responded had he been with David Richmond, Franklin McCain, Joseph McNeil and Ezell Blair Jr.—the original four demonstrators—in 1960 when segregation was in force?

"I would have gotten very, very angry," he says, and then pauses and reflects. "Well, I guess it's really hard to say what I would have done. I'll have to say those four guys did a pretty brave thing coming in here like that."

At another section of the counter, manager Moye gives permission to a young black journalist from the *Charlotte Observer* to take photos of the counter. Moye is friendly but somewhat guarded. He will not let visiting reporters interview waitresses, some of whom were there on February 1, 1960, including Geneva Tisdale, who is black and was nine months pregnant at the time. Curley Harris sent her home, afraid that the tension may cause her harm.

Harris has steadfastly refused to be interviewed through the years, usually hanging up when reporters call. He responds, "I didn't want to talk about it then; I don't want to talk about it now." (More than twenty years later, just before his death, Harris did give the *News & Record* a lengthy interview.)

The store has been busy this week, the twentieth anniversary of the sit-ins. ABC News has contacted Moye. A reporter from the *Los Angeles Times* bureau in Atlanta called to say that a team was headed to Greensboro. "Calls are coming in constantly," Moye says.

Paradoxically, Greensboro, which didn't invite publicity during the actual sit-ins, now embraces major anniversaries, such as the twentieth. The four original participants come back, sit at the counter and place an order. Ralph Johns, a white merchant who ran a store on East Market Street that catered to black college students and who promised the four bail money if they got arrested (they didn't), makes an appearance, as do other local black leaders. Woolworth's usually sends a vice-president from New York.

"We are looking at this thing as something positive," Moye says. "We don't see anything negative. We are proud we were the first" in downtown Greensboro to break with segregation.

Woolworth's, at the time, left decisions to integrate or segregate up to store managers. Stores outside the South were integrated; those in the South maintained a separate stand-up lunch counter for black customers.

It was as if in the 1950s, downtown merchants didn't want black people to venture across the railroad tracks that separated the city's black and white sections. But Jim Crow vanished quickly, and today many downtown merchants cater their advertising toward black customers.

Originally published in 1980.

Author's note: At the thirtieth anniversary in 1990, a plaque to the Greensboro Four, as they are now called, was placed in front of the store and their footprints were embossed in the sidewalk. Sycamore Street, beside the store, was renamed February 1 Place. David Richmond died in 1990, but the other three survive. In 2009, Franklin McCain was appointed a member of the board of governors, the body that governs the sixteen-campus University of North Carolina system. The Woolworth's store closed in the mid-1990s. It was expected to reopen in late 2009 as the International Civil Rights Museum.

HOUSE ON GTCC CAMPUS
STILL STANDS AFTER 180 YEARS

Jamestown—From 1926 until 1955, the first thing people did when they saw the white house looming beside High Point Road was to roll up the car windows. It served as a symbol of sorts for what stood behind it—the Guilford County Tuberculosis Sanitarium, where those with the contagious disease were sent for lengthy stays.

The simple Quaker-style house is nearly 180 years old, but it is best known for its uses in the past 70 years. A sanitarium doctor used it as a home. The first principal of Ragsdale High School, which opened in 1959 across the highway, lived there for four years. A secretary to the various presidents of Guilford Technical Community College (GTCC), which now occupies the sanitarium campus, lived in the house. Professors used it for offices. The drama department stored costumes and props there.

The house and the cute gazebo with green tile roof nearby remain as the only reminders of the sanitarium, which a Guilford County commissioner once called "as gruesome as the dickens." The county chose the site for the community college once the sanitarium closed in 1925. Classes were held in the hospital buildings until one by one they were all replaced.

The surviving house has far more significance than its connection to a hospital and college. It dates to about 1826 and—according to research by the GTCC History Club and a paper written by local historian Shelly Lutzweiler—is one of the oldest buildings in the county still at the same location.

The builder, Mark Iddings, was the son of Joe Iddings, and Mark's house was part of his father's farm. The father's house, stood nearby

This house, one of the oldest in the county, was built about a mile from Jamestown in 1826 by Mark Iddings, a farmer. *Photo by Jim Schlosser.*

on the same side of the road, now called the High Point Road if you live in Greensboro and the Greensboro Road if you live in High Point. According to the club's research, Joe Iddings was a first cousin of General "Mad" Anthony Wayne, one of General George Washington's top commanders in the American Revolution. Wayne is said to have stayed overnight at Joe Iddings's house and presented the family with one of his uniforms. Iddings's descendants later donated the uniform to the Greensboro Historical Museum.

When Joe Iddings died, Mark Iddings inherited the farm. His father had gained it through marriage to the daughter of Jonathan Howell, who owned the land that's now the GTCC, Ragsdale and Millis Road Elementary campuses. According to the History Club, Mark Iddings used bricks from his father's house for the foundation of his own home, where his eleven children lived on the upper floor.

GTCC history professor Jeff Kinard and History Club president Lisa Yeager point to a brick in the foundation with 1783 etched on it. They believe it may have come from Joe Iddings's house. "Today, you can stand outside and look one way and see the future of Guilford County," Kinard said of the campus, where students learn skills for future jobs. "And you look the other way at the house and see the history of the county."

The Iddings House beside the gazebo to the old tuberculosis hospital, the only surviving structure built by the hospital. *Photo by Jim Schlosser.*

The History Club wants to make the public aware of the house and to encourage the college to use it more. It has been inactive for periods, although recently lectures and receptions have been held there, including History Club meetings.

Kinard said that for a long while his experience with the house was like that of so many other High Point Road travelers. The house hugged the side of the road but didn't register. Perhaps that's because the house doesn't look that old after modernization and expansion in the 1950s and 1970s.

Preservationists say it is one of Guilford's most important old houses. A large fireplace, once open on both sides of the large front, was probably a key feature in a tavern that Kinard and Yeager believe was one of the house's many uses, although there is some disagreement on this. If a tavern, it would have served travelers on horseback and in stagecoaches between Salisbury, nearby Jamestown and the relatively new town of Greensboro, founded in 1808.

"This was a pretty lively place back then," said Kinard, peeking through a window at the front of the room. He said that the window replaced the tavern door. Outside, two large stones remain from what he believes were steps to the door.

Astonishingly, the house lacks honors. It isn't a county historic landmark or on the National Register of Historic Places, even though it qualifies. But it's safe from demolition. County commissioners placed a deed restriction on the house protecting it in perpetuity.

Originally published in 2006.

IS IT "MON-TI-SEL-LO"
OR "MON-TI-CHEL-O"?

Monticello—The only answer to the question is one your mother always gave: "Just because." A reader called up wondering why the little community of Monticello, in northeast Guilford County, pronounces its name Mon-ti-sel-lo. Why not Mon-ti-chel-o, the way Thomas Jefferson's mountaintop estate near Charlottesville, Virginia, is pronounced?

The reader could have as easily asked why Beaufort, North Carolina, is pronounced "Bow-fort" and Beaufort, South Carolina, puts the emphasis on "beau," as in "beautiful," which sums up both coastal towns.

The caller could have asked why Worcester, Massachusetts, is pronounced "Wooster." Just because.

As for the village of Mon-ti-sel-lo, "it's just always been pronounced that way," said lifelong resident Luke Lambeth. "It looks to me like it should be pronounced that way instead of Mon-ti-chel-o."

Kim Curtis, a media spokeswoman at historic Monticello, says that Thomas Jefferson had reason for preferring the Italian pronunciation, Mon-ti-chel-o, over the Anglicized Mon-ti-sel-lo. "Jefferson was fluent in Italian," she said, "and we believe that this is the way he said the name of his home." Also, Monticello's design had an Italian influence. When Jefferson began planning his estate in 1768, he was inspired by the work of sixteenth-century Italian architect Andrea Palladio.

Two villages offer choices for pronunciation. *Photo by Jim Schlosser.*

Curtis says that Guilford's Mon-ti-sel-lo isn't alone in its pronunciation. Some Monticello communities in the United States say it the same way, while others go with the Jeffersonian pronunciation. She says that even some locals in the Charlottesville area insist on saying Mon-ti-sel-lo.

It seems that if residents of Guilford's Monticello chose to name their village after Jefferson's home, they'd pronounce it the same way Jefferson did. *The North Carolina Gazetteer*, a book by historian William Powell about the name origins of nearly every city, town, crossroad, river and major creek in the state, says that Guilford's Monticello changed its name to honor Jefferson's home. That apparently came in about 1854, when the village opened Monticello Academy, which attracted students from all over the area. Until then, the community was known as Lambeth. The community has always been full of Lambeths.

Maybe the people of Monticello, where tobacco has been grown in abundance, as well as smoked and chewed, wanted to avoid a fancy Italian pronunciation. People might say folks here were putting on airs.

The lesson: pronunciation can be tricky and cause embarrassment.

For years, a man who drove U.S. 64 to the Outer Banks passed through a tiny community with a sign spelled Conetoe. He figured it was pronounced just as it was spelled, only to be embarrassed later when locals corrected him. It's "Ka-neat-ta."

Frankly, folks in tiny Monticello don't seem to care much if strangers say Mon-ti-chel-o instead of Mon-ti-sel-lo. It's a different story across U.S. 29, which separates Monticello from a community whose name has been feuded over for years and which newspapers get right about 50 percent of the time. Is it Brown Summit, Brown's Summit or Browns Summit? Officially, it's Browns Summit, although highway directional signs say Brown. The community is named for a farmer, Jesse Brown. The summit comes from the village being the high point on the railroad from Danville to Greensboro. Why Browns Summit? Just because.

Both Browns Summit and Monticello seem to be growing. It could be said that they are experiencing a "ren-e-sants." Or is "ri-nas-sant"?

Originally published in 2006.

OAK RIDGE HORSE SHOW ON AN UNUSUAL HOLIDAY, EASTER MONDAY, KEEPS GUILFORD COUNTY IN TOUCH WITH OLD SOUTH

Oak Ridge—It's events like the Oak Ridge Horse Show that reassure one that many southern values—fresh air, pastoral settings, country music, politicking and good company—still linger as society urbanizes.

The thirty-eighth annual Oak Ridge Horse Show started in almost perfect spring weather this morning on the grounds of Oak Ridge Elementary School, in this little community in northwest Guilford, best known as the home of Oak Ridge Military Academy. About one thousand people were in the bleachers for the start of the show at 9:00 a.m. The number was expected to escalate to ten thousand by noon, when a horse–country music pageant gets going.

The early arrivals were mostly show participants and their families. Riders were dressed in old-style English outfits featuring tight coats, sharply tapered trousers, knee-high black boots and black burgle hats. They curried and talked to their horses.

Several riders took horses through fast-paced practice workouts in the three rings used in the show. Other riders took their horses to the portable blacksmith shop operated by Ervin Beck of Winston-Salem. Beck, the stereotypical-looking blacksmith, sports huge forearms and rough skin. He travels the horse show circuit year-round. "I guess I'll show fifteen or twenty horses before the show ends tonight," he said as he dipped a burning shoe into a cooling pot.

While Beck worked and the riders made last-minute preparations, vendors and fiddlers set up shops and stages about the grounds, which had the look of an old-timey circus.

A scene from the Oak Ridge Horse Show, probably in the 1960s. *Courtesy of* Greensboro News & Record.

All types of horses high stepped about—big, little, black, white, gray, brown and spotted. More knowing horse people present called these horses English, Appaloosa, Western, Tennessee Walking, Palominos, pleasure horses, ponies and others. A few old dirt mules loosened up for their segment of the show.

The show has long been a fixture on Guilford County's spring social scene, the horse lovers' equivalent of golf lovers' Greater Greensboro Open PGA Tour tournament, which is held about the same time ten miles away. (The tournament has been moved to August.) The two events don't compete because the horse show is held on the Easter Monday holiday. Easter Monday is one of North Carolina's quirks. It and the Virgin Islands are the only places that observe it as a holiday, instead of Good Friday.

While the show has gotten fancy, the idea for it was conceived during World War II by men sitting around a potbellied stove in J. Frank Linville's store across from the Oak Ridge school grounds. "The men were trying to figure out some way to build a new Methodist church for the community," recalls Clarence Browning, a show official for twenty years. "Someone suggested a horse show and everyone agreed it might not be a bad idea."

A youngster in the 1960s wrestles a calf at the Oak Ridge Horse Show. *Courtesy of Greensboro News & Record.*

It was a poor idea, judging from the first show, in 1945. About one thousand people attended and the show generated about $1,000, hardly enough for a stained-glass window. But the show took hold, people came from afar and within a few years the Oak Ridge United Methodist Church was finished and stands as a memorial to the show.

Profits have proliferated. According to Browning, they now go into a special fund for the volunteer fire department, the little leagues and various other Oak Ridge community activities.

D.L. Donnell Sr. of Oak Ridge directed the show for many years before yielding in 1962 to R.N. (Buster) Linville, Oak Ridge's best-known politician, a former county commissioner.

In the beginning, there were few competing horses. This year, more than six hundred are expected, their owners coming from nearly every southern state.

The show has become a must place to press the flesh for Guilford County politicians, especially in election years. Those who don't spend most of the day kissing babies, pumping hands and acting if they are having a great time risk the wrath of voters at the polls in northwest Guilford County. "This is not even an election year but they will be here anyway," says Clarence Browning, adding that invites had been sent to the district's congressman, the state's governor and others. Congressmen are easy catches, but governors present a challenge. The last to attend was Governor Luther Hodges back in the 1950s.

Wouldn't you know it, "it was one of those miserable rainy days," Donnell said. "The show was called off but someone forgot to tell the governor. He pulled up in the parking lot in his limousine and not a soul was in sight. Boy was he mad."

Originally published in 1983.

A GUILFORD COUNTY CHURCH, FOUNDED BY A FORMER SLAVE, IS LINKED TO POET LONGFELLOW

Whitsett—The poet Henry Wadsworth Longfellow wrote, "All things come round to him who will but wait." After 130 years, recognition has arrived for Wadsworth Congregational Church, in the tiny Wadsworth community of eastern Guilford County. The county commissioners have just proclaimed the church as Guilford's newest historic site.

The narrow, white frame church with Gothic windows and a roof cupola looks lifted from a New England town commons. It's the kind of church Longfellow knew growing up in Maine and later when penning poems in a house near Harvard College in Cambridge, Massachusetts. The poet, who was white, and the Wadsworth congregation, whose approximately seventy members are black, are linked through William Madison Lindsay, who founded the church in 1870. As a slave, Lindsay had fled eastern Guilford years earlier for the North. He wound up in Cambridge, where, church members say, he worked as Longfellow's valet.

Longfellow is famous for his epic poem "Evangeline" and for shorter works such as "Paul Revere's Ride," whose opening line, "Listen my children and you shall hear…" has been recited by generations of American children. The same is true of Longfellow's "The Song of Hiawatha," which goes "By the shores of Gitche Gumee, By the shining Big-Sea-Water…"

The poet opposed slavery. He wrote *Poems on Slavery* in 1842. His best friend was U.S. senator Charles Sumner of Massachusetts, who, after making an antislavery speech, was beaten by a cane-wielding South Carolina senator.

Longfellow is said to have sent Lindsay to Oberlin College, an exclusive school in Ohio that accepted runaway slaves and free black people. The Oberlin College archives include a card for a "William Lindsey," a student from 1862 to 1866, but the document reveals nothing about him. Oberlin began as a Congregationalist school. It would be logical for a graduate bent on starting a church to associate it with the Congregational denomination.

After the Civil War, Lindsay returned to his native South and Guilford County and started Wadsworth Congregational under a grape arbor. He named the church in honor of Longfellow's mother's family.

Local historians have been slow to discover Wadsworth Congregational, perhaps because it is in extreme eastern Guilford, a section that has only recently begun to grow. The quaint little church stands out in the rural landscape when motorists crest a hill on Rock Creek Dairy Road.

Members of the congregation believe that Lindsay is buried in the church cemetery. Years ago, vandals broke the stone that may have been his marker. Weathering has obscured the stone's inscription, including dates. Church members aren't sure when the founder died, but he was still the pastor as late as 1900. Bob Jones, chairman of the church board, says that most of what the congregation knows of its history is unwritten.

Wadsworth Congregational Church, founded in 1870 by former slave Madison Lindsay, in eastern Guilford County. *Photo by Jim Schlosser.*

"It was all handed down from our parents and our grandparents," said Jones, who owns a real estate agency in Greensboro, thirteen miles away. Gloria Whitted, a church board member, scolded herself recently while walking from the wooden church to a brick structure in front that replaced the old church in the 1970s. (The old building remains in use for special occasions.) "I wish I had asked them more questions," seventy-one-year-old Whitted said with despair.

Her late grandmother and aunt knew Madison Lindsay. So did Ibie Dick, a former slave who was still alive when Whitted was a child. "She used to tell us about slavery," Whitted said. "She said as a little girl she would climb up in a tree with a book so the master wouldn't see her."

The presence of former slaves in a small community probably meant that a plantation operated in the area before the Civil War. Older residents remember a large, abandoned house that had belonged to a white family named Foust. A 1796 Guilford County map names a John Foust in the area. It was common for slaves to adopt the last name of their owners. The names stuck and were passed on to descendants. Gloria Whitted's maiden name is Foust.

Madison Lindsay may have belonged to the white Lindsay family, who was instrumental in the founding of Guilford County in 1771 and Greensboro in 1808. The original Lindsay plantation was near Jamestown, in western Guilford.

Willie Breeze Jr., a church board member who prepared Wadsworth's application for historic status, is a Lindsay through his mother. Lindsays remain in Wadsworth, but Breeze believes he may be from a different branch of Lindsays than the ones near Jamestown. A file on the white Lindsay family at the Greensboro Public Library reveals that Samuel Lindsay settled in the vicinity of Wadsworth Church. Curiously, the white Samuel Lindsay had a son named J. Madison Lindsay. William Madison Lindsay, the Wadsworth pastor, married Lettie Morehead. Perhaps she was once a slave owned by the family of John M. Morehead, governor in the 1840s. He lived in Blandwood Mansion, now a National Historic Landmark in downtown Greensboro. Morehead was known to have had slaves.

The white Moreheads and Lindsays were related by marriage. Members of the two families, Lizzie Morehead Lindsay and Lettie Morehead Lindsay, have almost identical names. The white Moreheads and Lindsays also were related to the Robert Dick family of Greensboro, who lived at Dunleath, a Greensboro mansion that the Yankees occupied at the end of the Civil War. Many black people with the last name Dick live in Wadsworth.

Church members realize that research needs to be done to sort out the church's and the community's past. A National Park Service administrator at the Longfellow National Historic Site in Cambridge could find no mention of Madison Lindsay working for the poet. But, the administrator said, the Longfellow family had servants and Lindsay could have been one of them. Long ago, the church had a school that had a bell that now belongs to a Girl Scout camp in Guilford. But Wadsworth's church bell remains in the cupola of the old church building belfry. The historic designation signals that Wadsworth Congregational Church has not only been there a while but also intends to stay put, despite all the growth around it. "God has protected this church this long," Breeze says. "He will continue to protect it."

Longfellow would have likely viewed Wadsworth Congregational Church as Madison Lindsay's life's footprint. The poet once wrote, "Lives of great men all remind us. We can make our lives sublime and, departing, leave behind us, footprints on the sands of time."

Originally published in 2000.

THE CITY'S PIPING PROUDLY
ABOUT ITS ANCIENT WATER PIPES

Next year, during Greensboro's bicentennial, it would be revealing if the lid was lifted off the city's landscape and everyone could peek beneath. They'd see an incredible maze of pipes, some old enough to have earned the status of museum pieces. In 1986, the city removed a piece of the still functioning water main three feet under Elm Street and sent it to the Iron Pipe Century Club, sponsored by the Ductile Iron Pipe Research Association. The organization honors pipes and other public works machinery that last one hundred years or more.

The Elm water main was about to turn 100, as was the line it served. The now 120-year-old line, which as best can be determined still carries water we drink, runs along North and South Elm from Bellemeade Street on the north to Lee Street on the south. Workers found the date "1887" stamped on the pipe. That meant that installation came during the reign of Mayor Robert King, whose administration began the city's water system between 1882 and 1888.

There's more than just pipe beneath downtown and the suburbs. If the city wants to run streetcars again, the tracks from old remain. Electric streetcars went into use in 1902. They eventually ran from downtown to White Oak, Irving Park, Pomona and other places. When the system shut down in the 1930s, the tracks were left and paved over. Sections of rail occasionally reappear when crews dig up streets. The city is now spending $50 million to replace a sewer line installed in the 1930s from the North Buffalo Waste Treatment Plant to about Hill Street at the end of Latham Park.

Melinda King, a city engineer who is the project's manager, says that the 1930s line replaced one installed in 1918. The 1918 pipe remains in the ground, she says, and so will the 1930s' pipe. It's cheaper to let old pipe stay buried rather than dig it up and haul it away. Archaeologists could dig downtown and hit a network of pipes that, in the late 1800s and well into the twentieth century, carried what was called "manufactured gas" to light streets, businesses and homes in the center city. The gas came from heating coal. This was done at a manufacturing plant located at what is now the intersection of East Friendly Avenue and North Church Street. Cleaner-burning natural gas later made manufactured gas obsolete.

As for the new sewer line in the Latham Park area, the old line must be replaced because it leaks sewage during heavy rains. The city got more than seventy years of use from it. Not good enough. The city believes that the four-mile line would have lasted longer if it had been made of more lasting ductile instead of concrete. The replacement will be ductile. King, the project manager, says that the new line should be good for at least one hundred years. That means that it will be ready for replacement when Greensboro celebrates its 300th anniversary in 2108.

Originally published in 2007.

HUMPHREYS FOLLY
FOOLED EVERYONE BY LASTING

When First Citizens Bank broke ground this week for its four-story Greensboro headquarters at the southwest corner of Elm and Market Streets, the question was whether it would outlast the building it replaced.

Nearly 150 years ago, in the early 1830s, when Greensboro was about 25 years old, businessman Henry Humphreys built the village's first "high-rise." It towered three stories in a town where the few commercial buildings stopped after one story. "It was the talk of the town," says Karen Carroll, an archivist at the Greensboro Historical Museum. "People were saying, 'You shouldn't build a building that high.'" Especially in a town that was still considered backcountry, with no guarantee it would succeed.

Because the locals were convinced that the building was doomed to fail, they dubbed it "Humphreys Folly." The name stuck, and to everyone's amazement, so did the building. It wasn't torn down until the late 1960s, with a drugstore that formed a triangle with its front door facing Elm and Market remaining a popular hangout to the end. Even after demolition, the building's columns remained for several years. It turned out that they were holding up a building next door. The columns looked lovely, and until First Citizens got around to building, the place was called First Citizens Plaza. Public and private ceremonies were held there.

Wednesday afternoon, as work began on the First Citizens Building, the few remains of Humphreys Folly confounded men in bulldozers who were hitting the brick foundations. "This makes the work a lot harder for us," said Julius Rankin Jr., who is grading the site for a McLeansville company.

An early photo of Humphrey's Folly. *Courtesy of Greensboro Historical Museum.*

Rankin knows old buildings. He snared a loose brick and broke it in half. "This is homemade brick," he explained. "You can tell it's not pressed good inside like modern brick. This brick is old."

In a few more days, all traces of Humphreys Folly will be gone from Elm and Market, the intersection where the first courthouse was built after county commissioners moved the county seat in northwest Guilford, site of the 1781 Battle of Guilford Courthouse, to the closest spot in the county's center they could find. But the Humphreys's legacy won't entirely vanish. Humphreys's heirs saved a forty-foot strip on the tract and are leasing it to the bank. A local real estate agent, Charlie Weill, said that he sends the rental check to two heirs, Winder Hughes Sr. of Wilmington and Margaret Lee of Stamford, Connecticut, both in their nineties.

"There may be some families out in the county with longer ties to a piece of property, but inside Greensboro I don't know of anyone else who goes nearly that far back," said Weill, who, along with his late father, goes a long way back in Greensboro's real estate business.

After the nickname Humphreys Folly finally died out, the building was known by various names through the years, including the Wynne, Klutz and Taylor buildings.

For much of the building's history, the ground floor had a drugstore. It was known for a long time as Liggett's drugs and, until recently, Lane

Rexall Drug, which has moved down and across South Elm Street. All the drugstores had marble soda fountains. The places were coffee-sipping places for businessmen, lawyers and the two famous cops, Sunshine Wyrick and "Double A" Hall, who tried to unsnarl Elm and Market traffic.

In the 1920s and 1930s, the well-known New York stock firm Bache & Co. had its Greensboro office in the Folly. The Art Shop, still in business out in the suburbs, was there for years. Marine Corps recruiters signed a few good men in the Folly. The Pink Lady Beauty Salon also was there. The building, especially the drugstores, drew customers from neighboring businesses along West Market, such as Acrobat Shoe Store, which sold Poll Parrot shoes for children. Henry Humphreys died in the 1840s and is buried in the venerable Buffalo Presbyterian Church cemetery.

Humphreys Folly wasn't his only contribution to Greensboro. In the 1820s, he opened the Mount Hecla factory downtown, the state's first successful steam-driven cotton mill.

The name folly didn't fit Humphreys. Records at the Greensboro Historical Museum show that he owned real state in the village worth about $12,000. That doesn't sound like much now, but in Humphreys's time, the whole city was valued at $58,000.

Originally published in 1983.

A STRUCTURE ARCHITECTS WON AWARDS DESIGNING IS GONE IN SECONDS, BUT SYMBOL OF BURLINGTON INDUSTRIES BUILDING LINGERS IN DUST

Winners and losers stood out Monday after two hundred pounds of synchronized explosives collapsed the headquarters of once mighty Burlington Industries on West Friendly Avenue. Thousands of spectators gathered at nearby Friendly Shopping Center felt the ground shake and heard a series of ear-hurting booms. They watched as the 430,000-square-foot building seemed to break in half and fall. It was all over in seconds.

Throughout, the spectators cheered and hollered. A huge cloud of black and white smoke arose from the blast site, hiding the ruins of the former six-story building. Smoke and dust drifted east toward the shopping center. Eye rubbing commenced, but not all was dust related. Emotions had kicked in. Many onlookers had worked for Burlington Industries when it was the world's largest textile company. Its headquarters, which at one time had 1,250 employees, was considered a showcase example of modern architecture in North Carolina. It won five awards for the architectural firm of Odell & Associates of Charlotte.

While the demolition crews celebrated with backslaps and embraces, Burlington's former employees looked as if they had lost a young friend. The building lasted only thirty-four years, replacing a once grand headquarters downtown built at the height of the Depression and serving as county social services headquarters for decades after Burlington left. Also looking gloomy were those associated with people who had spent two years building the headquarters, which opened in 1971.

"I'm here representing my father and grandfather," said Charles Bryce Isom, who was seven when he moved to Greensboro from California with his father, the late Charles B. Isom, and his grandfather, the late Charles F. Isom. His grandfather came as general superintendent for Daniel Construction Co. and his father as ironworks foreman. "I'm glad my grandfather is not here to see it come down. The building was a great source of achievement and pride to him," said Isom, a Greensboro police detective. He brought along scrapbooks that included photos of him as a boy playing among the massive steel trusses that held the building in place until 10:00 a.m. Monday.

David Griffin Jr., who runs the demolition company D.H. Griffin with his father and other family members, said that it was a "textbook" takedown of a difficult building. The structure was loaded with steel trusses, some weighing forty-eight thousand pounds each.

But not everything went perfectly. The blast sent debris flying across West Friendly Avenue, slightly injuring one man and damaging a window of a house in the Wedgewood neighborhood. Griffin said that some flying debris was expected. Houses on the northern side of Wedgewood stand three hundred yards from the building and were in the unsafe zone. Griffin said that employees had gone from house to house warning residents to stay inside or leave temporarily.

It was obviously a big day for Griffin's group, which had its own production company photograph and record the implosion. "Ready to go. This is what we work for," declared Griffin worker Dave Dundas as zero hour approached. His T-shirt identified him as "Demolition Dave." While a fire engine sounded siren blasts at two minutes, one minute and fifteen seconds before demolition, Marylene Griffin knelt over a small square box on the asphalt outside the Grande Theater. After a worker counted down to zero, her push of a button sent an electrical charge through one thousand feet of yellow wire stretching to the building. The electricity set off blasting caps on four hundred charges in holes that welders had opened in the steel trusses. From the first explosion, it took about twelve seconds to obliterate a once celebrated example of modern architecture.

D.H. Griffin Co., founded in 1959, averages about twenty implosions a year, but this was the first button push for Marylene Griffin, wife of demolition company founder D.H. Griffin. She had worked at a now closed Burlington Industries plant on South Elm Street.

This was the largest implosion in Greensboro since 1971, when a thirteen-story building downtown, a luxury hotel gone to seed, went down.

"It's a sad birthday for me; I'm seventy-eight today," said Mae Carroll, who started with Burlington in 1946 at its former downtown headquarters and came to the new building on West Friendly Avenue at a time when the company employed eighty-five thousand people at plants worldwide.

Asked what Burlington's fiery founder, the late J. Spencer Love, would think of the demolition and the troubles—mainly overseas competition—that have reduced the textile maker into a shell of its old self, Carroll replied, "If he were still here, this would not happen." Love, who died more than forty years ago, would have devised a way to compete against the cheap foreign textiles that doomed so many American textile companies, Carroll said.

Regardless of why Burlington declined, "It's a memory that is going to have to die," said Donnie Goldston, the building's engineer from 1973 until Burlington moved out last November. He served as a consultant to Griffin on the demolition.

The name Burlington Industries has almost disappeared, along with its local competitor, Cone Mills Corp. The two companies have merged and the office staff works in Green Valley office park, not far from the fallen former headquarters. The merged company is called the International Textile Group.

Fred Ayers, a veteran construction man who works in Florida and was a top Daniel Construction person on the Burlington job, flew to Greensboro to watch the end. "An explosion that big has to be impressive," he said. Even so, he said, "it's a sad moment." Continuing, he said, "Everyone has a resistance-to-change function in them."

After the site is cleaned up, a new shopping center will be built as an associate of neighboring Friendly Center.

Originally published in 2005.

HEROES, CHARACTERS, A CELEBRITY

A BLACK HERO AMONG WHITE SOLDIERS
AT GUILFORD COURTHOUSE

G eneral Nathanael Greene, sword-swinging giant Peter Francisco, Lighthorse Harry Lee and a few other American warriors hog the attention during recounts of the Battle of Guilford Courthouse in 1781. Rarely does the name of an enlisted man from Maryland, Thomas Carney, get mentioned, even though he contributed mightily in what history calls a "Victory in Defeat."

The American forces technically lost the battle waged over one thousand acres in what is now northwest Greensboro. But Greene's soldiers killed and wounded so many enemies and so weakened the British that they effectively destroyed the Redcoats as a fighting force. The English surrendered more than six months later at Yorktown, Virginia.

Carney is credited with killing seven British soldiers in hand-to-hand combat. Yet, while founders of Greensboro named the town for General Greene and later streets and apartment complexes honor Peter Francisco and even a main thoroughfare is named for the arch enemy, British commander Charles Cornwallis, nothing recalls Carney's deeds, at least until now.

The lack of recognition may have resulted from Carney being an enlisted man, although Peter Francisco was also a private. But Francisco was an oddity, a giant at six feet, six inches, who killed eleven British soldiers with his sword during the battle. One other characteristic may have denied Carney recognition: he was black, a rarity in the American Continental army.

The ranger staff at Guilford Courthouse National Military Park, which covers about one-fifth of the battlefield, has decided that it's time Carney got

Thomas Carney, a black man who fought heroically in 1781 at the Battle of Guilford Courthouse during the American Revolution. The drawing is by Don Long, a ranger at Guilford Courthouse National Military Park, based on his research on Carney, who was from Maryland. *Courtesy of* Greensboro News & Record.

his due. Ranger Don Long has used his imagination to make a drawing of how Carney might have looked.

Long became aware of Carney a few years ago while sifting through research compiled by a local chapter of the Daughters of the American Revolution.

The ranger learned that Carney had joined the Seventh Maryland Regiment at the start of the Revolution in 1775. He fought at the Battle of Germantown, Pennsylvania, under General George Washington and encamped with Washington's forces during that frigid winter at Valley Forge.

Carney was still with the Marylanders six years later, in the slave-owning South, when his unit joined other American Continental units and the ragtag, untested, untrained North Carolina militia to confront the world's greatest army in the wilds of central North Carolina. The battle site was in and around a little village, now vanished, called Guilford Courthouse.

"Greene posted the Maryland Brigade in a strong line between...the North Carolina and Virginia militia," Long wrote in a recent report for the park's Black History month observance. "The British easily pushed aside the weaker militiamen...The elite British Guards and the Marylanders collided."

Carney, Long wrote, valiantly cut down Redcoats in bayonet fighting. "The brave and determined stand in the face of the British juggernaut," Long wrote, "allowed the rest of Greene's army to make an orderly withdrawal, saving it to fight again."

After Guilford Courthouse, Carney saw action at a battle in Ninety Six, South Carolina, where he pulled his wounded commander off the battlefield to safety before collapsing, exhausted.

After the war, Carney returned to Maryland, apparently to farm. A Maryland newspaper in 1829 reported that "Thomas Carney, a colored man, age 74, died near Denton, Md., 30 June." The obituary told of Carney's wartime gallantry.

The library at Denton, on Maryland's eastern shore, showed that he received a postwar pension that amounted to half his pay as an army private.

Carney's great-grandson, Horace Noble Carney, a retired postal worker in Germantown, Pennsylvania, where soldier Carney once lived, said by telephone that he had no idea his great-grandfather had fought in the American Revolution. "It makes me quite proud," he said. He went on to say that sometime between 1800 and 1810 Carney married Anna Winter. They had two sons, Levi and Thomas Jr. Levi was Horace Noble's grandfather.

Ranger Long says, "It has only been in the last twenty years that an effort has been made to establish what role black people played" in the war. "If you ask the average guy on the street did they know about blacks in the Revolutionary War, they will say, 'No, it was all Paul Revere and the Minutemen.'"

But the fact is that slave owners sent slaves to fight as substitutes, including a slave named Ned Griffin of Edgecombe County, North Carolina. The master promised Griffin his freedom in return for fighting, but the master reneged on the promise after the war.

Long says that a Rhode Island unit was made up almost entirely of black soldiers, and Massachusetts had an all-black unit. They fought even though it was a war to win independence for American whites. But Long says that perhaps the contributions of black soldiers hastened the end of slavery in the 1860s.

Of the many monuments in the park, one honors Maryland's soldiers, but no individuals are cited.

"The Marylanders were definitely the best of the American troops in the battle," Long says, "and they were equal to or better than the British army."

With guys like Thomas Carney carrying the muskets, it's no wonder.

Originally published in 1985.

THE *MASH* MAN, DR. JOHN LYDAY, SERVED IN TWO WARS—AND AS THE MODEL FOR TRAPPER JOHN

Few people who saw the retired doctor spending his last years tinkering with a twenty-year-old Cadillac Seville or working in his garden knew of his connection to one of Hollywood's funniest films and TV series. Nor did many people know the horror that Greensboro surgeon John Lyday, who died Monday at age seventy-eight, had witnessed in two wars, as an enlisted man in World War II and as an army doctor in Korea.

It was in Korea, while serving with the 8055th Mobile Army Surgical Hospital, that Lyday worked alongside another surgeon, Dr. Dick Hornberger. Using the pen name Richard Hooker, Hornberger later wrote a book based on his experiences. It became the smash hit antiwar movie *MASH* in 1970, and the movie in turn became a TV series from 1972 to 1983.

Though Hornberger borrowed pieces of personalities for characters, he had Dr. Lyday in mind when he created Trapper John, played in the movie by Elliott Gould and on TV by Wayne Rogers. "He was the prototype for Trapper John, the one who had the baby back home. I was that little baby," said Carolyn Lyday, the doctor's daughter, who teaches at the George School, a Quaker preparatory school near Philadelphia. She was six months old when her father went to Korea.

Lyday never boasted of his connection to the book, movie and series, and he wanted nothing to do with being a celebrity. However, when actor Loretta Swit, who played Major Margaret "Hot Lips" Houlihan in the TV series, came to Greensboro years ago, Lyday appeared with her on the *Good Morning Show* on WFMY. He also attended reunions of the 8055th with Hornberger.

Carolyn Lyday says that her dad had a dry sense of humor and realized that the movie and show *MASH* used dark humor to illustrate war's wretchedness. But he never laughed about anything related to combat. His daughter says that tears would well up in his eyes when he recalled World War II. He had seen comrades blasted out of the sky in planes flying next to him. He was a technical sergeant who had left Western Carolina University after two years in 1941 to join the army, where he became a gunner and radioman on B-24s in the 445th Heavy Bombardment Group. He flew thirty-two missions in Europe, where he won numerous combat medals, including the Bronze Star, the Distinguished Flying Cross and the Air Medal.

While returning to England after a mission in heavy fog, Lyday's plane lost the use of its altimeter. The pilot and copilot had no way to judge the plane's altitude. "They didn't know if they had the right altitude to make it over the cliffs of Dover," Carolyn Lyday says. "They made it."

After the war, Lyday says, her father "felt he was a very lucky man. He wanted to make his life count."

Between the wars, Lyday finished undergraduate studies and medical school at UNC–Chapel Hill (which then had a two-year medical program) and went on to earn his MD at the University of Pennsylvania. After Korea, he returned to the University of Pennsylvania to complete his surgical internship and residency. The medical school offered him a teaching post, but he wanted to return to his native North Carolina.

He had grown up the son of a farmer in Pisgah National Forest, in Transylvania County near Brevard, where his grandfather and a brother were doctors. Dr. Russell Lyday, a Greensboro surgeon and an older cousin, invited John Lyday to join his practice in Greensboro in 1958. Together, the two Lydays spanned the history of Moses Cone Hospital. Russell Lyday was Cone's first chief of surgery when the hospital opened in 1953. John Lyday served as Cone's chief of surgery from 1973 to 1975.

"He was tough, loyal, honest as the day is long and conservative," said Dr. Robert Phillips, Lyday's friend and his predecessor as chief of surgery at Cone. "He was someone you could count on all the time." Phillips says that he regrets talking Lyday into retiring in 1989 after Lyday developed lung cancer. Lyday made a complete recovery, and Phillips says the doctor could have kept on practicing another eight or nine years.

But his family says that Lyday enjoyed his retirement, working on old cars, especially the Seville, and in the garden.

Originally published in 1999.

A MAN FOR ALL HISTORY

Who will D'oyle Moore awaken as today? General Nathanael Greene? Daniel Boone, who once lived in the state? Calvinist Jonathan Edwards? Edwards's seventeenth-century sermon, "Sinners in the Hands of an Angry God," gets Baptist preacher Moore's juices flowing when he delivers such lines as "There is no want of power in God to cast wicked men into hell."

Moore is for hire to play, at last count, forty characters from the Revolutionary and colonial periods. Besides Greene, Boone and Edwards, his characters include George Washington, Patrick Henry and Kings Mountain fighter William Campbell. He does about a dozen preachers, among them early Guilford County leader David Caldwell, renowned orator George Whitefield and Old Salem founder Bishop Spangenberg.

During the Greensboro bicentennial in 2008, Moore and his wife, Janet, logged countless hours wearing ungodly hot outfits that Nathanael Greene and wife, Caty, sweated in more than two hundred years ago. Moore loves being told, "You look and act like you just stepped out of the eighteenth century." He takes pride in immersing himself "in the mindset of our forefathers."

He says that he feels more comfortable in that period. He wishes that he could have preached during the "Great Awakening," which featured hell, fire and brimstone revivals by Whitfield and others along the East Coast. Besides the pulpit, these men preached from the saddle in fields. Moore does that on his horse, Coosau. He's also mounted when he plays the part of Peter Francisco, the giant swordsman at the Battle of Guilford Courthouse in 1781.

Although Moore and his wife get paid—about $500 a day plus expenses—they view their work as a calling to keep eighteenth-century history and preaching alive. "Every program is fresh, new and different," he promises, "like I've never done it before. I'm not a cookie cutter."

For years, he was a standard coat-and-tie preacher, as well as a carpenter. In the 1960s, he did the interiors of many houses in fashionable New Irving Park. He took his first step back to the eighteenth century thirty years ago when he inserted an apostrophe in his name to make it look like and reflect his Ulster-Scot background.

He first performed as David Caldwell in the mid-1990s at, where else, the private David Caldwell Academy. The location was fitting because Moore dates his love of the eighteenth century to a fifth-grade state history class at another David Caldwell, a now closed public elementary school in south Greensboro.

Boyhood visits to Guilford Courthouse National Military Park, where General Greene confronted British general Cornwallis, increased his fascination with the era and characters in the battle. He spent hours as a boy in the old main library reading about colonial history. Seated in a library Windsor chair, with light coming through the arched windows, the atmosphere felt like the eighteenth century. The former library buildings, more than one hundred years old, are now the Greensboro Historical Museum.

Brought up Baptist on the city's south side before his parents moved to the upscale Starmount-Hamilton Lakes area, Moore, now sixty-eight, became a Baptist student minister preaching at small churches. He did so while attending Mars Hill, then a two-year college, and later Greensboro College. He was one of the first men to attend the previously all-female Greensboro College. He later went to theological school in Texas. He preached off and on, did carpentry and studied history on his own.

Moore always wears carefully reconstructed eighteenth-century garb when speaking before a group. He wears the outfits when he does weddings, funerals and other religious functions as well. He says that he normally makes one appearance a week, sometimes two or three. He has appeared in six documentaries and is working on a book about some of his characters. Janet Moore also is available for solo performances as Caty Greene and Rachel Caldwell (David's wife). She is researching Abigail Adams and also writes children's books.

D'oyle Moore as General Nathanael Greene during Greensboro's bicentennial parade in 2008. *Photo by Jim Schlosser.*

The couple lives in a two-room log cabin in Stokes County while awaiting completion of a new, old-looking house near Walnut Cove. They moved from Summerfield in Guilford County for eighteenth-century reasons. "We had to get deep into the woods," Moore says during a day off, wearing regular work clothes and cowboy boots. Besides, they needed a wardrobe room. Their uniforms include a bedraggled single shirt and breeches of a poor colonial farmer and Greene's elegant blue and buff uniform, which doubles as George Washington's garb. Moore only has to change the sash and the epaulets on the shoulders to make Washington a three-star general. Greene had two stars. Moore estimates that he has $3,000 invested in the uniform. Just the gold bullion epaulets cost $300 to $400. He saves money on other uniforms. Janet Moore, in addition to having a doctorate in English from the University of Nebraska, is a seamstress. She makes his shirts and breeches and most of her dresses.

At the urging of the military park staff in Greensboro, Moore added Greene to his repertoire eight years ago. He played Greene in the movie *Another Such Victory*, which is shown at the park's visitors' center. He also makes a cameo as Greene's opponent, Cornwallis.

As for his favorite character, Moore gives the diplomatic "whoever I'm playing" answer. "If I have to single out one that I'm more alike in character and look alike, it's probably General Daniel Morgan," he says of the Revolutionary War hero of the Battle of Cowpens in South Carolina. When the History Channel aired a show on Morgan about five years ago, at the end Moore rode through smoke toward the camera. As he got closer, a portrait of the real Morgan slowly came into focus. It was hard to tell the two apart.

For his monologues, Moore's research relies on libraries, scholars and visits to historic sites. He loves visiting public schools, where children always ask, "When did you die?" He replies that he knows he did die but can't remember anything about it. He's done some dying—forty times so far.

Originally published in 2008.

GUILFORD'S FIRST AND ONLY FIRST LADY

S he was the most popular and fashionable first lady of them all—and her first name wasn't Jackie. Dolley Madison might not have been as dashingly chic as Jacqueline Kennedy, but she was as much admired and had every bit as much style, charm and penchant for fine things.

To have seen the bejeweled Dolley in her French-made gowns dancing at her husband Jimmy's inaugural ball or calmly evacuating the White House as the British approached—it would have been hard to believe that this sophisticated woman was born in a log cabin in woods off what is now West Friendly Avenue in the Guilford College community.

Tonight, some 250 patrons of the Greensboro Historical Museum will see a private preview of the museum's newly renovated Dolley Madison exhibit room. They will see the former first lady's gowns, chain, slippers, postcards, Bible, a handwritten poem, mother-of-pearl snuffbox and two Mathew Brady photographs taken when she was eighty and still wearing black thirteen years after her husband's death.

The Dolley Madison collection—considered the most extensive in the country—was purchased in 1960 by a group of Greensboro residents and donated to the museum. The four-hundred-item collation cost $10,000—the buyers called it a steal.

The items to be displayed represent a portion of the collection. In the museum's vault are such treasures as a coded letter that James Madison, the nation's fourth president, wrote to his successor, James Monroe. And the collection grows. Recently, museum director Bill Moore returned from

A drawing of Dolley Madison, born in Guilford County before it was founded in 1771. *Courtesy of Greensboro Historical Museum.*

James Madison's native Virginia with brace irons that held the smoldering logs that warmed James and Dolley at Montpelier, their Virginia estate.

On Sunday, the Dolley Madison exhibit opens to the public after being closed for a year. Before, museum visitors had to stand in a doorway behind a rope to view artifacts. Now, they will be able to enter the chandeliered room. New wall panels trace Dolley Madison's life from New Garden, now Guilford College, to Virginia to Philadelphia to Washington. She presided over grand parties, set fashion standards for the era and served the first ice cream in the White House.

"She was a hostess in the best sense," says historian Gayle Fripp of the museum staff. "She made people feel comfortable of all political persuasions. She represented something very sophisticated, very fine in Washington at a time when it was a primitive place."

Not by coincidence, Sunday's reopening falls on Dolley's birthday—her 216th.

Granted, Dolley Madison lived in what is now Greensboro only for the first nine months of her life. But that is enough for Greensboro to claim her. Forget that for years the street signs near her birthplace said "Dolly Madison Road." Dolley—with an "e" please—never revisited the area, but she knew from whence she came. "She said she was born in North Carolina but she gave the wrong year," director Moore says. She liked 1772 better than the actual year of her birth, 1768.

A plaque in the yard of a brick house in the 5500 block of West Friendly Avenue is the only reminder, besides the street name, that the first lady once lived nearby. Her family's cabin stood about one to two hundred yards behind the house. "We employed some archaeologists in 1971 to examine the site," Moore says. "They dug some trenches but couldn't find anything."

Historians, however, are certain of the location. They are convinced because of recollections handed down through several generations of Guilford College area residents. In the 1840s, former New Garden (now Guilford College) Boarding School president Nathan Hunt showed the cabin to his students. At the time, Dolley Madison was America's most famous woman.

The cabin was torn down before the turn of the twentieth century, but a few logs help hold up a rustic structure on the historic museum grounds.

Dolley's parent left New Garden, a Quaker community, for Virginia and eventually settled in Philadelphia. There she married John Todd, and they had two children. Todd died of yellow fever in 1781. A year later, widow Todd married U.S. representative James Madison, forty-three, of Virginia, who had helped write the Declaration of Independence.

Madison became president in 1809. To celebrate, his wife organized the first really splendid inaugural ball. Once in the White House, she spent months decorating. She insisted on American-made furnishings while continuing to order her own clothes from Paris. She gave parties and luncheons, writing the invitations herself.

During the War of 1812, when the British burned down the White House, Dolley Madison escaped with the famous Gilbert Stuart portrait of George Washington, although some historians now question whether she really did.

A daguerreotype of Dolley Madison as an elderly woman. *Courtesy of Greensboro Historical Museum.*

After James Madison's death in 1836, widow Madison was reduced to poverty by her son, Payne Todd, a card-playing gambler and boozer. Dolley spent $30,000 covering his debts. Dolley liked cards, too, but she gave up playing because she didn't think it was a proper activity for her, says historian Fripp.

Dolley Madison managed to keep up appearances. She moved in 1837 to Lafayette Square, near the White House. Her sitting room stayed filled with guests. Her social calendar was thick with galas and ceremonies, including participating in the groundbreaking of the Washington Monument.

In February 1849, five months before her death, she made a final public appearance. She was the guest of honor at the first presidential reception of President James K. Polk. She looked as refined as ever as she entered on President Polk's arm as the Marine Corps Band played. It was a fitting end for Dolley Madison—she, a North Carolinian, arm in arm with Polk, a North Carolinian born near Charlotte.

Originally published in 1987.

GREENSBORO'S FIRST EAGLE SCOUT
NOW A CENTENARIAN

G reensboro—That Harry Neel became the first ever Eagle Scout in Greensboro in September 1921 amounts to an incredible honor in itself. What may be more amazing is that Neel, fifteen at the time, is still alive to tell about it. He turned one hundred in May. He says that he's slowed only slightly since he visited Greensboro in 1999 to be honored at the Old North State Council's Eagle Recognition Banquet.

The new Royce Reynolds Family Scout Building off Westover Terrace maintains a display case honoring Neel. It includes his Eagle badge. The retired surgeon, who after completing medical training at the Mayo Clinic settled in nearby Albert Lea, Minnesota, says that he had "a little trouble" last year and had a pacemaker installed. "But I keep house and have a garden," he said. "I go to the Rotary Club meetings and some church meetings." When he arrives at those gatherings, people sometimes ask how he got there. "I tell them I drove my car here," he said. He also has a Ford pickup that he drives around town and to his small farm outside of town.

Neel has been pretty much away from Greensboro since 1924, when he went off to Washington and Lee College and, later, to Johns Hopkins Medical School and the Mayo Clinic. He practiced medicine until his late seventies in Albert Lea, population about twenty thousand, or about the size of Greensboro when Neel was a boy.

Upon returning to his hometown in 1999, he was totally lost. Greensboro had sprawled into a city of more than 200,000. He stayed at the Battleground Inn on Battleground Avenue. The avenue had been a dirt road when he was a

Above, left: Harry Neel as a teenager after becoming Greensboro's first Eagle Scout in 1921. *Courtesy of Old North State Council, Boy Scouts of America.*

Above, right: Harry Neel, the city's first Eagle Scout, still flying high as he turned one hundred in 2006. *Courtesy of Old North State Council, Boy Scouts of America.*

Boy Scout. His troop, under Scoutmaster Frank Casper, hiked the road from downtown on field trips to Guilford Courthouse National Military Park.

As a teenager, Neel watched Greensboro develop a skyline. He remembers bleachers at Elm and Market Streets, from which "sidewalk superintendents" like himself watched the seventeen-story Jefferson Standard Building go up in the early 1920s, the South's tallest building for a brief time.

Neel attended the city's first graded public school, Lindsay Street, which opened in 1870 and closed in 1925.

Neel was five and living in Asheville when his father died of tuberculosis. The next year, Harry and his mother, Bessie, moved to Greensboro, where she went to work for the Internal Revenue Service. That year, the federal income tax was started.

They lived at the Benbow Arcade, a large building with apartments and single rooms for rent in the 200 block of South Elm. He loved living in downtown Greensboro, across from the city's major department store, Meyer's. He spent hours at the YMCA, then on South Greene Street, a block from the Benbow. It had a gym and indoor pool. Greensboro High School, then on Spring Street downtown, played its basketball games at the Y. Neel won the city table tennis championship at the Y and was a leader throughout the city selling war bonds during World War I.

Neel says he had two goals in life as a youth: to be a Boy Scout and a doctor. The day he turned twelve and became eligible, he joined the Scouts. The Boy Scouts originated in 1907 in Great Britain, with the Boy Scouts of America organized in early 1910. Greensboro's first troop, Troop 1 at First Presbyterian Church, came later that year. When Neel sought the Eagle badge—Scouting's highest rank, earned by only 2 percent of Scouts—he was helped by Casper, who seemed to spend more time on Scout work than his job making mattresses. Neel recalls that Casper would pick him up early in the morning in his Ford to go study birds as one of the Eagle requirements. Neel also had to do a distance run in a certain time. Casper paced him in the car. The newspapers hailed Neel as the city's first Eagle Scout.

Neel hopes to make another trip to the city. He's got time. His mother, who later moved from Greensboro to Albert Lea to be near her son, lived to be 103.

Originally published in 2006.

A VIETNAM TRAGEDY

When Billy Wayne Flynn was nine years old, he told his Aunt Ruby that he was going to attend the U.S. Military Academy at West Point. Ruby Dowling wanted Billy to dream big goals but felt that it was her duty to tell him about the sad reality. "Billy Wayne," she said, "you'd better get that out of your head. Only rich people go to West Point." She knew that Billy's parents and other family members lacked the political connections she figured were needed for admission to the academy.

Billy's father, Sankey Flynn, labored at Cone Mills. Billy's mother, Majorie Flynn, worked at the soda fountain at Edmunds Drug Store in Summit Shopping Center. The couple lived in a mill house at Summit and Nineteenth Streets in the mill-owned White Oak Village. They knew no one in Congress who could sponsor Billy.

Even before he mentioned West Point, his parents say, he showed a fascination with the military. He spent hours lining up toy soldiers. As it turned out, the boy wasn't engaged in a wild childhood fantasy. Flynn did become a West Point cadet. He got to the academy in a roundabout way, one of the few to do so without a high school diploma. He graduated in the class of 1966, later profiled in the best-selling book, *The Long Gray Line*. Of the 579 class members, 30 were killed in Vietnam and more than 100 would be wounded. No other class suffered more casualties than that of '66. Billy Flynn was the first from the class to die, only seven months after graduation.

Flynn, with blond hair, a radiant smile and an eagerness to volunteer or try out for any activity, will be in the thoughts of family and old friends today, as Memorial Day honors Americans who served in war.

A reminder of how long Flynn has been gone—thirty-three years—came last week when a Greensboro foundation announced a $1 million donation to help build the Kathleen Price Bryan Family YMCA downtown. The new Y will be in the 500 block of West Market Street, where the YMCA stood before it moved to its present site in 1969. That old Y was Billy Flynn's home away from home as a boy. He was a Y counselor and lifeguard.

After Flynn's death in early 1967, the Y decorated its big meeting room with his portrait and named the room for him. Flynn's portrait also decorates the living room wall of Sankey and Majorie Flynn's small apartment on Summit Avenue, where the couple, now in their eighties, moved from Nineteenth Street six years ago.

By the time Billy Flynn was a teenager, he was the type of boy a military academy or any college would love to enroll. He won awards for delivering the morning newspaper. During youth week at Sixteenth Street Baptist Church, he preached the Sunday sermon. When Page High School opened in 1958, Flynn played on the school's first football team; wrote and edited for *Pages by Page*, the student paper; helped the community by joining the service-oriented Key Club; and brought home honor-roll grades. Classmates and teachers were shocked when, halfway through his junior year, the seventeen-year-old Flynn quit Page and joined the army as a private. The decision devastated his parents and aunts. They had looked to Billy as the family's bright and shining hope. Neither of Billy's parents nor any of aunts had finished high school. They didn't want another dropout in the family. "But he had his mind made up," his mother says.

By then, young Flynn perhaps realized, as his aunt had years before, that he didn't have the connections needed to enter West Point if he had stayed at Page. But army recruiters had told Flynn that if he enlisted, he might earn an academy appointment for deserving young soldiers in the ranks. In the army, Flynn became a paratrooper. The army saw his leadership potential and sent him to an army prep school at Fort Belvoir, Virginia, to compete with others for a small number of academy appointments.

In early 1962, Billy called the drugstore to tell his mom the news. He had won an appointment through the army and through the sponsorship of Representative Horace Kornegay of Greensboro.

The four years when Flynn was at the academy were joyous for his parents. They visited the spectacular West Point campus on the bluffs above the Hudson River. During one trip, they met legendary General Douglas MacArthur. They watched on graduation day as Billy and his classmates performed the traditional toss of the caps. The next day, Flynn served as best man at the wedding of fellow cadet John Lester. Flynn had a sweetheart, too, a young woman he had met at an academy dance. They became engaged but broke it off before graduation.

As if the paratroopers and West Point weren't enough of a challenge, Lieutenant Billy Wayne Flynn volunteered next for the Rangers, the toughest of the army's elite outfits. Training included living in swamps and forests and eating whatever he could hunt. After completing Ranger training that fall, Flynn was ordered to Vietnam, where American involvement was building. First, he came home for a brief visit, and family and friends found him to be the same old Billy: modest and eager to help.

Before departing for Vietnam in December, Flynn telephoned his mother at the drugstore. He wouldn't quit talking, she remembers. It was just about small stuff. "Son, we are talking long distance!" Marjorie Flynn declared. "Write me a letter."

If she had known it would be their last conversation, "I would have talked all day," she says. Flynn sent a long, upbeat letter from Vietnam. He hadn't seen combat yet and said that Vietnam duty so far was like a vacation. He announced that his former fiancée had written to patch things up. She promised to wait for his return.

Flynn always had his life mapped out. In the letter, he revealed his plans for after Vietnam. He intended to go to army foreign language school and then return to West Point to teach. After that, he would seek a post at the Pentagon.

During this period, Sankey Flynn's father—Billy's grandfather—was ill. When a car pulled into the Flynns' driveway in late January 1967, Majorie Flynn thought that it might be bad news about old Mr. Flynn. But when two grim-looking army lieutenants came to the door, she knew that it was about Billy. She tried to slam the door, as if that would make the bad news disappear.

The officers had no details of how Lieutenant Flynn had been killed. The family later learned that a Viet Cong sniper in a tree had shot Flynn in the neck, killing him instantly. Flynn was wearing a black armband so soldiers would recognize him as company commander. The sniper apparently knew the band's significance and honed in.

When Sankey Flynn, who served in the navy in World War II, overheard the lieutenants say that his son was dead, he began walking in circles. He

A portrait of the late Billy Flynn, after graduation from West Point, hangs in the lobby of the Kathleen Edwards Bryan Family YMCA. *Courtesy of Bryan Family YMCA.*

did so for days. Right after Billy went overseas, Sankey Flynn had dreamed of his death. Later, when he heard how Billy died, it was exactly like the dream, he says.

The body came home and the parents went to Lambeth-Troxler Funeral Home for a farewell look at their only child. Worried about how his wife would react when the casket was opened, Sankey Flynn says, "I was ready to grab her because I was sure she would fall. She didn't." "The Lord was holding me up," Majorie Flynn says.

Billy's parents at first lamented the cruelty of losing their son after he had worked so hard for his goal. The Lord's ways are mysterious, the family says. Billy was taken, but a cousin sent to Vietnam was spared. "If there is anything to God choosing people to come to heaven to help him," says one of his aunts, Ellen Jordan, "Billy would have been one of them."

The Flynns thought about having Billy interred at the cemetery at West Point but picked Greensboro's Westminster Gardens instead. They visit his grave often and place a flag there each Fourth of July.

When Flynn's uniforms and possessions were returned, his parents kept his medals and hats but gave the rest of his uniforms to Billy's best army friend, John Lester. Lester, who died in 1994 in California, named his first child after Billy Flynn.

The Flynns sent Billy's class ring to West Point, where it's displayed with rings of other distinguished West Point graduates. Someone told the Flynns that the ring is close to General Dwight D. Eisenhower's and MacArthur's rings.

Originally published in 2000.

Author's note: After Flynn's death, Sixteenth Street Baptist printed a booklet with the sermon he had preached as a sixteen-year-old.

MOSES WAS MARRIED HERE

The couple looked like typical sightseers admiring a pretty church. He was pointing. She was clicking her camera. But the tall man's commanding presence was unmistakable. A pedestrian along West Friendly Avenue downtown was on target when he declared, "Hey, isn't that Charlton Heston?"

The Academy Award–winning actor who rode the chariot in *Ben Hur*, descended from the mountain in *The Ten Commandants* and barked orders as the circus boss in *The Greatest Show on Earth* returned to Greensboro Thursday with his wife, Lydia, for the first time in forty years. They came from California to campaign for Republican candidates Ronald Reagan and Jesse Helms Jr. and to engage in romantic nostalgia by visiting Grace United Methodist Church.

Their visit was also a reminder of Greensboro's World War II history, when a temporary Army Air Corps base on the edge of downtown brought thousands of fresh recruits for basic training and, later, for last-minute training before deploying overseas. Heston was just another private hoisting an M-1 rifle, doing jumping jacks and being yelled at by drill sergeants who had no idea, of course, that they were cursing a future onscreen Biblical figure.

"It had a blue ceiling when we got married. It's white now," the actor said, emerging from the church in a bright red shirt. "There was a flowering cherry [tree] over there," said Lydia Heston.

It was a rainy day, March 17, 1944, when Heston and Lydia Clarke wandered through downtown looking for a place to become husband wife.

Charlton and Lydia Heston in 1984 outside Grace United Methodist Church. *Courtesy of Greensboro News & Record.*

He had just finished training at what was then called Basic Training Camp 10 (BTC-10), located on nearly one thousand acres behind what's now Northeast and Summit shopping centers on Summit Avenue. She was a student, as he had been, at Northwestern University near Chicago.

They knew no one in the city. Heston found a jewelry store that he believes was near the old King Cotton Hotel, perhaps the city's most elegant lodging place then. He bought a ring, saying, "I remember I got it for twenty-one dollars." They picked Grace Methodist after entering it to get out of the rain. Charlton Heston was enchanted by the blue ceiling.

They found two women working in the church kitchen who agreed to be witnesses to the wedding. The minister, Emmett McLarty, was summoned to make the man and wife pronouncement.

At the church on Thursday, Dorothy Poer, one of the witnesses, who had gotten word that the Hestons planned to visit the church, returned and stood in the doorway to greet them. They embraced, and the eighty-three-year-old Poer accompanied the couple into the sanctuary, just as she had in 1944.

Later, Lydia Heston went across Friendly Avenue to take photos of the church from different angles. "Isn't this just marvelous," she declared.

Unlike that day four decades before, this autumn day was spectacular. Earlier, at the hotel near the Four Seasons Town Center, where Heston spoke to the political gathering, he took credit for the weather. After all, he's Moses. "Don't clap," he deadpanned. "It's not that hard really. It just takes a little concentration."

Lydia Heston also spoke, answering the question on everyone's mind: how can any Hollywood couple stay married forty years? "The secret," she said, "is love."

Originally published in 1984.

RICH NO MORE, BUT HAPPIER

John Lindley III, an hourly wage worker, held the plumb bob on a crew doing survey work on Camden Road in western Greensboro. Suddenly, he realized that at that moment a bank was auctioning three large parcels belonging to his late and once rich father, Jack Lindley Jr. Some of the land had been handed down during the past one hundred years by the family patriarch, the first John Van Lindley. He had been one of Greensboro's wealthiest and most respected men in the late nineteenth and early twentieth centuries.

As he thought sadly about the auction, Lindley III could see a sign of his great-grandfather's legacy. He looked away from the plumb bob, across Camden Road, at Lindley Elementary School, built in 1922 and named for the first Lindley. So was the surrounding Lindley Park neighborhood, in which Lindley III's surveying crew was working. So was the Lindley Park recreation area with its walking trails and ball fields. So was the nearby Lindley Park municipal pool. So was the former Lindley Junior High School, now converted to apartments that include the old main building. The first Lindley was the only man to have had two Greensboro schools named for him. For decades, you could say the name Lindley and no more was needed. The family ranked with the mill-owning Cones and landowning Benjamins as the city's wealthiest. John Lindley I had started Lindley Nurseries before the Civil War. Business was interrupted during the war while the Quaker and antislavery Lindley left to go join the Union army. He returned after the war and none of Greensboro's many Confederate vets seemed angry with this "scalawag," as Southerners called those from Dixie who served the North. Lindley built Lindley Nurseries into one of the largest in the Southeast.

When his grandson Jack, formerly named John Van Lindley II, gained control of the business, the family was phasing out the nursery. The nursery's vast land, stretching from the Pomona community on the west side of Greensboro out to the Friendship community in western Guilford, was more valuable than the nursery business. In Friendship, Greensboro had started its municipal airport in the 1920s. It was initially called Lindley Field (now Piedmont Triad International Airport) because the strip was on nursery property.

Jack Lindley added to the acreage and also inherited and increased the family's stockholding in Jefferson-Pilot Life Insurance Co., now Lincoln Financial. Although a man with a reclusive nature, Jack Lindley served on the city council and held other offices. He was mysterious about his doings. He preferred doing deals from phone booths, and also from a telephone in a downtown florist shop whose founders had once worked for the nursery. Lindley III eventually joined his father's one-man operation in a small office in the Jefferson Standard Building. Jack Lindley rarely showed up at the office and rarely confided in his son, who had made law review at UNC–Chapel Hill before quitting in his second year because of depression and other personal problems.

The Lindleys for many years lived in a magnificent house bordering the fifteenth hole of the Greensboro Country Club. Lindley III developed a golf game that included tee shots that flew longer than many PGA Tour players. He went to good schools, prepping at the exclusive Woodberry Forest School in Virginia before attending UNC as an undergraduate and, for two years, at the university's law school. When Jack Lindley died in 1990, his son thought that he stood to inherit millions.

Now, it's apparent that the unsettled estate may be $10 million in debt. Lindley III has had to move out of Irving Park, drop out of the country club and give up other luxuries. He has been living in a motel for transients along Interstate 85-40 and has learned to be a surveyor to support himself.

He wants no pity. He enjoys working for Robert E. Wilson, Inc., surveyors, which used to do work for the Lindley family's landholdings. Robert Wilson and his son, Alan, hired John Lindley III last May when he was as down as he could get. "I absolutely love it," Lindley says of the job. "The only thing you have to worry about are the yellow jackets and mean dogs."

"When he talks about his work, he really becomes animated," says his wife, Chris Lindley, who is separated from John (they later divorced) but remains close. "That is the joy of his life." He has given up wearing a suit and tie to work for brogans and jeans. His surveying team includes instrument operator Dennis McIntosh and crew chief Max Moody. The other day, at a subdivision under construction near the Oak Ridge community in northwestern Guilford County, McIntosh was looking into the surveying instrument while giving complicated hand signals to Lindley, who was standing down the road with a plumb bob.

"It has taken a lot of fortitude for him to come from his background to this line of work," Moody says. "I really respect him." McIntosh said, "No briers are too thick for him, no creek too deep. He just jumps right in. He will do everything you ask of him. He's just a real great guy and a friend, and he has a great sense of humor."

That sense of humor returned only recently. The past three years since his father's death were nightmarish for Lindley, who had worked for his tightwad dad for seventeen years, never making more than $36,000 a year. The elder Lindley was reluctant to sell land. He preferred to use it as collateral to buy more property. Without Lindley III knowing it, Jack Lindley borrowed against the land and his Jefferson stock to pay bills that the younger Lindley didn't know existed. Jack Lindley then borrowed more to pay interest.

Lindley III knew about some debts but figured that his father's overall holdings far exceeded what his father owed. That was true for a while, but the recession of the late 1980s caused Lindley land to plummet in value. Despite his flaws, Lindley Jr. was a visionary. He saw the increasing value of land near the airport and bought more. He also was a behind-the-scenes broker in a deal that merged a Greensboro bank with a Charlotte bank. The new bank became North Carolina National Bank, then NationsBank and now Bank of America.

When Lindley III tried to talk his father into settling some debts, the elder Lindley stalled. He would sell only at the eleventh hour when a lender threatened legal action. When Lindley III warned his father about how debt could pose a future problem, his father always said, "We'll worry about that when the time comes." Jack Lindley had battled his way out of the Depression during the 1930s. He figured that he could handle these modern times.

After his father died, Lindley III realized that debt overwhelmed their assets. The attorney for the Lindley estate said recently that the estate might show a small surplus once everything is settled. Lindley III hopes so, but he doubts it. He estimates the deficit at $10.5 million. He expects not a dime.

Lindley III suffered a heart attack on Christmas Eve 1990, two months after his father's death. Later, he went into a deep depression. In late

1992, his two-year marriage broke up, though he and Chris see each other often. "She has been a great support to me during these trying times," John Lindley says.

He reluctantly consented to an interview, declaring, "With the exception of my father, no one hates publicity more than me." He feels the need to set some matters straight, however. He wants to stifle rumors that he's ill and unable to function. He has never felt better physically, he says. People who have known him for years remark that he looks fit and much slimmer. The outdoor work has revitalized him and elevated his self-esteem.

Lindley wants bankers and creditors to know that "I want to pay my dad's debts, my debts and make sure mother is taken care of. I say give us enough time, and we'll pay you back to the best of our ability."

His eighty-two-year-old mother resides in WellSpring, a Greensboro nursing home. She has little money besides Social Security and some rental income. The banks could go after the rental properties.

Lindley says that he should have been more forceful with his father. A passive nature is part of his personality and perhaps his Quaker heritage. (He is now a Presbyterian). "He kept me at arm's length," Lindley says, adding that in essence he had no real job during the time he worked for his dad. He didn't even know of his father's whereabouts much of the time. "He might drive to Raleigh to see someone, but that person wouldn't know he was coming and wouldn't be there," the son says.

The elder Lindley might then catch a plane in Raleigh to Charlotte to see more people who might or might not be there. He'd then fly back to Raleigh to fetch his car. He never wanted anyone to know where he was and was addicted to using pay phones. "He knew every booth between here and Raleigh," Lindley says.

Going from paper millionaire to near pauper might destroy most people, but John Lindley seems to have adjusted. Besides, he says, he and his father never felt rich even when they were. "That is the saddest thing," Chris Lindley says. "They never enjoyed the money when they had the money."

"I really admire John the way he has handled this thing," says Carl Carlson III of Bankers Trust. "When people are backed up against a wall, their real characteristics come out. John's characteristics are all you could ever hope for in a human being."

"I have never seen anyone so humble," Chris Lindley says. "He was that way when he had money. He's that way when he doesn't have money." As a surveyor, he enjoys being out among the deer tracks with his friends at the surveying company. Looking back, he wishes that he had studied forestry in college. But he's looking forward, not back.

"I'm doing fine. I love what I'm doing now," he says. "But I don't like owing money."

Originally published in 1993.

Author's note: John Lindley III died on April 15, 2009, at age sixty-six. His father's estate remains unsettled after all these years, but it did not produce any income for John III. After retiring from surveying in the early 2000s, he lived in a cluttered apartment in Latham Park surviving mainly on Social Security and help from wealthy friends he had grown up with in Irving Park, who took turns checking on him at his apartment.

A POET'S LOVE LETTERS TO HIS WIFE

I t's enough to break your heart on this Valentine's Day.
Mary V. Jarrell attended a lecture at a book club recently and heard a professor say that poems about love and beauty—the kind that John Keats wrote and Jarrell's husband, Randall, penned occasionally—have been out of style in academic circles for years.

Passion is passé? Romantic musings aren't right with the times? Not as far as Mary Jarrell is concerned. She won't accept that readers desire a loveless society; maybe it's just that many of today's writers do. She wants to read love poems and love stories. Her late husband, Randall, loved love, too, and expressed it even when mental demons tortured him.

Now regarded as one of America's outstanding twentieth-century poets, Randall Jarrell wasn't swayed by shifting literary winds. His widow says that he paid no attention to critics who sighed that he was too sentimental when he wrote about love and beauty and romance. "I think that a lot of people are starved for love poetry," she says.

And old-fashioned love letters, too, like those that Randall Jarrell wrote her before and during their marriage. It was during the romantic 1950s, at a writers' conference in Colorado, that Mary von Schrader of California met the dashing poet Randall Jarrell. His interests included translating Goethe from German, playing tournament tennis, collecting *Road and Track* magazine, driving fast cars and teaching English at the Woman's College in Greensboro, now the coed University of North Carolina at Greensboro.

Today, Mary Jarrell treasures the six-line love poem "Meteorite" that Randall Jarrell wrote for her after their romantic encounter in the Rockies:

Star, that looked so long among the stones
And picked from them, half iron and half dirt,
One; and bent and put it to her lips
And breathed upon it till at last it burned
Uncertainly, among the stars its sisters—
Breathe on me still, star, sister.

The meaning may puzzle readers, but to Mary Jarrell it's as clear as that summer day in 1951 when they hiked a dry creek bed near Boulder, Colorado, and she found what looked like a meteorite.

Earlier, Randall Jarrell had told her that his intellectual river had gone dry, like the creek bed. His literary essays and poetry had been praised by such intellectual giants as Edmund Wilson. But Jarrell confided that he hadn't completed a poem in months. He worried that he was washed up. Mary reminded him that he was only thirty-seven. His best writing was ahead. Before they departed Colorado, Jarrell asked her to marry him. Soon after that, "Meteorite" appeared in her mailbox in Pasadena. The poet explained how a meteorite burns out but ignites again as it passes stars while journeying through the universe. He felt that their time together in Colorado had restored his poetic flame.

He sent her letters that pointed to their past as proof that they were meant for each other. As youngsters, they had lived in Long Beach, California, at the same time, although they didn't meet. "I keep thinking of all the astronomical coincidences!" he wrote. "Our Oldsmobiles and both of them in 'sea-foam green,' and both of us in Long Beach at the same time and both of us born in 1914, both of us in early May. Truly, we are one and were always one. As you know, there is no difference between us, and we are each other's completely. Be mine forever as you are mine now and were always mine."

Whoooo! Cool this Cupid down! Mary von Schrader was right. Jarrell's best writing was ahead. In 1960, he won the National Book Award for his collection of poems, *Woman at the Washington Zoo*. Earlier, he served two years as poetry consultant to the Library of Congress, a position that evolved into poet laureate of the United States in 1984. His close circle of literary friends included Allen Tate, John Crowe Ransom, Peter Taylor, Robert Lowell, Robert Penn Warren, Karl Shapiro and Elizabeth Bishop, all great writers.

Randall and Mary Jarrell, who married in 1952, lived on Greensboro's Tate Street before moving in 1959 to a rustic house in the woods off New Garden Road, near Guilford College, a place so quiet that Randall Jarrell commented you could hear the fox say goodnight to the hare.

Mary Jarrell has been a widow now for nearly thirty-three years. Randall Jarrell was fifty-one in 1965 when a car struck him while he was walking along a dark highway in Chapel Hill. Mary continued to live in their home until three years ago, when she moved to the WellSpring retirement center. Somewhere in storage is the meteorite—not the poem, but the rock from that Colorado creek bed.

Early last year, a *New Yorker* magazine representative called Jarrell to say that she had read some of Randall Jarrell's love letters that are in the Berg Collection at the New York Public Library. She asked Mary Jarrell's permission to use excerpts in the magazine.

The August 25, 1997 *New Yorker* was devoted to love. It started with an essay by Louis Menand. "What all the world really loves is not a lover," Menand wrote. "It's a love story." Scattered among the articles were four of Randall Jarrell's letters and those of three other writers, including Simone de Beauvoir and Dylan Thomas. Two of the Jarrell letters were from May and August 1965, a time when the poet suffered inexplicable depression so severe that psychiatrists considered shock treatment. The depression changed his personality and hurt his marriage and relations with friends, who told him that he was magnifying his problems, making mountains out of mole hills. "When you're depressed, there are no mole hills," he responded. He didn't blame his wife for his melancholy. He made that clear in the May 1965 letter when he was hospitalized:

It's Sunday morning, and I've just looked at the roses you brought me from our own front yard, and put on the nice shoes you brought me—because of them I dressed entirely by myself—and now I'm writing this on the clipboard you brought me, and thinking of all the other things you brought me, that for so long made me better and happier, and kept something like this from happening to me earlier. You are the one big good real thing in my life, and I'm so glad I met you—we've had hard times.

In the August letter, he recalled one of those good times:

Each of us is the other's bluebird of happiness, but it's nice for us to have, for any wandering bluebird out in the world, a little brown house in a tree.

Mary Jarrell with a portrait of her husband, the poet Randall Jarrell, part of a mural in the Greensboro Public Library. *Courtesy of* Greensboro News & Record.

Remember the day when the whole flock of bluebirds spent the afternoon in our front yard? I hope they do again this fall, and hope that we'll be there together to see them. I've just been rereading some of the letters you've sent me, and I felt very happy and lucky to have someone to love me so and write me so. I love you.

After his death in mid-October, his friends speculated that he had lunged in front of the car. Mary Jarrell, though, is convinced that it was an accident, and the coroner who investigated agreed. She buried her husband in the New Garden Friends Cemetery near their home. The gravestone remembers him as "poet," "teacher" and "Beloved husband."

Jarrell is baffled that some feminists in academia bash her husband's work as antifemale. "He loved women," she says. True, he once wrote mockingly of the southern twangs and intellect of some of his Woman's College students. But he also wrote how bright others were. Jarrell says that female students eagerly signed up for his courses and many sent him valentines on this day each year. The poet loved receiving and sending cards, she says. "Silly ones, clever ones—he was a very affectionate man," she says.

She believes that he would be distressed by how few people take pen in hand today to write their own valentines, letters, love poems or any kind of message. They e-mail, fax and telephone love, she says. The few who still use pen and paper to express endearments wouldn't dare show the letters or poems to others, let alone a half-million *New Yorker* magazine readers. But Mary Jarrell doesn't mind blushing publicly about her years with Randall Jarrell.

"I like anything that keeps me still in contact with him, and these letters do that," she says.

Originally published in 1998.

Author's note: Mary Jarrell died at age ninety-three in 2002.

SWEET MEMORIES OF
HIGH POINT'S MUSIC MAN

The U.S. government has honored the late John Coltrane, the jazz legend who grew up in High Point, by designating his former home a National Historic Landmark. But this Coltrane house, sure to become a mecca for tourists, is in Philadelphia. It's not the one Coltrane grew up in at 118 Underhill Street in High Point.

The government's decision to grant landmark status to his Philadelphia house doesn't help High Point in its efforts to draw attention to its Coltrane connection. But there may soon be yet another Triad link to the jazz musician. Fans of the saxophonist say that the High Point Museum stands a good chance of getting a valuable collection of Coltrane memorabilia to attract visitors to his old boyhood haunts along East Washington Street in the Furniture City.

Coltrane's parents brought their three-month-old son to High Point from his birthplace, the North Carolina town of Hamlet, in 1926. He remained there until he was seventeen, when he and his mother moved to Philadelphia. He learned to play the saxophone while in school in High Point.

Coltrane graduated from the old William Penn High School, where he played in the school band, and he is said to have practiced ten to twelve hours a day. He also attended St. Stephens AME Zion Church, where his grandfather was pastor.

"He is the most undeveloped asset that Guilford County has, if you ask me," says John Morton, a Greensboro banker and longtime Coltrane fan whose goal is to increase local awareness of Coltrane.

The house in which John Coltrane grew up. High Point hopes to restore the house as a museum. *Courtesy of* Greensboro News & Record.

Today, thirty-two years after his death at age forty from a liver disease, Coltrane is literally worshiped—there's a church named for him in San Francisco—by jazz lovers who consider him a performing and composing genius. His compositions include "Cousin Mary," "Equinox," "Giant Step" and "Impressions." One of his best sellers was a recording of the popular song "My Favorite Things."

"Trane," as he was called, won a Grammy, was named Jazzman of the Year in 1965 and was inducted into the Jazz Hall of Fame a year after his death. Today, he ranks in the pantheon of jazz greats with Dizzy Gillespie, Charles Parker, Miles Davis, Thelonious Monk, Louis Armstrong and Duke Ellington.

Still, as recently as 1983, when the North Carolina General Assembly recognized Coltrane's greatness, few people in High Point and Guilford County had heard of him.

Morton believes that High Point still can become a must-visit location for Coltrane fans. He says that a collector in Osaka, Japan, is talking to the High Point Museum about donating his collection of Coltrane memorabilia. The museum is building a twelve-thousand-square-foot addition. The Osaka collection includes photographs, films, videos, letters and other items related

A bust of the jazz legend John Coltrane, who grew up in High Point. The sculptor, Gilbert Hines, stands next to the artwork. *Courtesy of* Greensboro News & Record.

to the musician. Morton says that Philadelphia deserves its claim on Coltrane, too, because, "this is where the world came to know him."

In Philly, Coltrane fell in with talented young musicians, Morton says. When he prospered, he bought a spacious, three-story town house in north

Philadelphia and lived there from about 1952 to 1959, when he moved to Huntington, Long Island. "A lot of the great music that we have come to know and love was produced in that house," Morton says about the home in Philadelphia. "The piano that he composed that great music on is in that house." Coltrane's cousin, Mary Lyerly Alexander, still lives there, Morton says. She inspired Coltrane's tune "Cousin Mary."

John Salmon, a music professor at UNCG and a Coltrane fan, speculates that racial segregation may be the reason Coltrane is better known elsewhere than in his old hometown. "High Point is always claiming Coltrane but the truth is he made a name for himself away from High Point," Salmon says. "High Point didn't do much for Coltrane during his lifetime." Until the 1960s, Morton says, Jim Crow laws would have prevented Coltrane from playing before an integrated audience in High Point or in nearby Greensboro.

Coltrane returned for visits but never performed here, Morton says. By the time of integration in the 1960s, he was playing all over the world and probably wouldn't have had time for an engagement in High Point or Greensboro, neither of which is a jazz haven. Morton blames ignorance of jazz, not racism, for High Point's lack of familiarity with Coltrane. If he had been a rock 'n' roll star, black or white, it would have been a different story, he says.

Morton and some friends founded the John Coltrane Commemorative Committee in High Point and were responsible for a memorial plaque installed at Commerce and Centennial Streets in 1996.

Coltrane's old house on Underhill, where he lived with his parents and grandparents, is privately owned. Morton sees little chance of it becoming a museum. "Coltrane is still a mystery in town, although not as much as he was ten years ago," says Morton, who first heard Coltrane's jazz as a college student.

A few of Coltrane's acquaintances remain in High Point. Rosetta Haywood was his classmate from the first grade on. She had no idea then that he would become famous, but now she understands why he did. "He was in the music room constantly," she says. "You would hear him all the time."

Morton said he believes that his High Point years influenced Coltrane. The tremendous passion and intensity with which he played may have resulted from the deaths of his father and grandfather a few months apart in 1938. Coltrane was close to both. Religion was a big part of his upbringing, and that also is felt in his music, Morton says. Some people say it's almost a religious experience listening to Coltrane. That accounts for the Saint John Coltrane African Orthodox Church, founded in 1971 in a San Francisco storefront. The pastor plays Coltrane jazz at 11:00 a.m. worship. "There is a very strong spirituality to his music that is deeply felt," Morton says. "It is like a prayer."

Coltrane waved off the analysts who wanted to parse his style, declaring, "I just play the horn hard." He once played a song for three straight hours. Miles Davis is said to have once told Coltrane how to end a song: take the horn out of your mouth.

John Morton plans to continue his mission of making Guilford County more aware of its famous son. Like listening to Coltrane music, he knows that it will take time. But there's no rush. "People will be listening to his music," he says, "a thousand years from now."

Originally published in 1999.

> Author's note: The City of High Point has since bought the Coltrane house on Underhill Street and hopes to make it a museum.

HE LIVED LIFE HIS WAY

After strangers encounter Preston Jones the first time, they want to shout out loud, "Did you see that old fossil?!" To people in their forties and fifties, the eighty-two-year-old Jones harkens hazy memories of great-grandfathers who lived on farms with the barest of comforts. To younger adults and teenagers, Jones is beyond comprehension.

He's never been to McDonald's. He lives in a tiny house with a tin roof and without running water off Coble Church Road in southeast Guilford County. An outhouse stands behind the house and a well in the yard. The well, he says, amounts to an upgrade from when he was a boy, when he walked a ways to fetch water from a spring. He cuts his own wood for heat and grows most of his food. He used to hunt for meat, boasting, "I never came in under one hundred squirrels a winter." He quit hunting because he fears that too many wild critters now carry rabies.

The youngest vehicle he has owned is his '66 Ford pickup, painted red, his favorite color. Before that, he drove a '37 Chevrolet car. The farthest north he's ever been is just over the Virginia line, once, to tow a friend's broken-down truck back to Guilford County. The farthest south is South Carolina, many years ago on a bootlegging mission. He says he never made illegal whiskey, "but my daddy did."

He was without electricity until he married sixty years ago. He outlived that wife, by whom he had four sons. His second wife died two years ago.

Jones's health began sliding a year ago. He came down with pneumonia, and later, a serious blood disorder was diagnosed, requiring frequent blood

Preston Jones lives primitively by today's standards, loves and doesn't fret that he has a life-threatening blood disorder. *Courtesy of Joseph Rodriquez of* Greensboro News & Record.

transfusions. "The doctor has looked him in the eye twice and told him he would die from it," says daughter-in-law Pam Jones, who lives across the road and up the hill from him. The dire words didn't seem to register, Pam Jones says. She isn't sure whether he comprehended or if he was ignoring the bad news. His doctor is amazed that Jones, despite a low blood-cell count that would keep others in bed, keeps puttering along, making only a few concessions to illness. "He used to get up at 4:30," Pam Jones says. "Now he might get up at 6:30."

His family and friends worry that others might be offended by an elderly man being allowed to live primitively. Thomas Neese, president of Neese Country Sausage, stresses that Jones "lives in the type of house he does by choice, not because he can't afford anything else. You can live in a log cabin and be as content as someone in a mansion in Irving Park." Jones worked for Neese Sausage for forty years and, until December, was still being summoned from retirement to work part time. Some people believe that Jones knows Neese's top-secret sausage recipe. Neese says that Jones knows parts of the process but not all. Only a few people do. Neese wishes he had the recipe for Jones's old-fashioned work ethic. "He's out of the old school," he says. "He believes if he's going to be associated with something, he's going to give it his all."

Jones is one of the few left who can remember Neese's grandfather, Theodore Neese, who co-founded the business with his son, Homer Neese, in 1925 and built it into a regional institution. "He was a fine fellow who walked around smoking one of those crooked pipes," Jones says of Theodore Neese, who used to stop Jones and other farm boys who were plowing with mules to chat. Old Man Neese loved to talk, he says. So does Jones, but when talk turns to how Neese Sausage is made, he shuts up. He worries that Neese's competitors might glean a secret out of anything he says.

He shows company loyalty by wearing a hat with Neese's name and logo, a pig. He's rarely seen in anything but bib overalls—low back only, Pointer Brand, from a store in Randleman that he switched to after prices rose at a store in Greensboro.

Although he won't say how sausage is made, he'll tell you how to grow cotton, which he picked as a boy on his father's twenty-five-acre farm near Julian, three miles away. He can tell you how to weave cotton into cloth because he worked twelve years at Cone Mills' former Proximity Mills in Greensboro before joining the sausage company.

His working life began at age thirteen, on a farm, not long after he quit school after four grades. "I thought I was one of the best ones in my class," he says, "but my teacher didn't like me. She treated me mean."

Jones misses plowing behind horses and mules. He loves animals, with the exception of red foxes, despite his fondness for red. Red foxes aren't native to the area. He remembers the man who long ago turned loose a bunch of fox pups in the woods to multiply for the pleasure of hunters. Red foxes have become so plentiful, he complains, that rabbits, which he once trapped, have about vanished.

As often is the case with people living close to the earth, wild creatures don't act skittish around Jones. Deer—he says he never saw one as a boy, but they are now everywhere—come up to him in the fall and eat persimmons from his hand. He gets mad when squirrels steal peaches from his tree. Still, the pesky little rodents make him laugh when they clutch a peach between their front paws and carry it across the road.

"Tell about your apple tree," his daughter-in-law urged him the other day during a talk at her dining room table. Jones beamed at the chance to tell of his miracle tree. It had refused for years to bear apples. He told a friend, who suggested that he drive a rusty nail into the ground at the base of the trunk. Jones did so last year. "I've never seen so many apples," he says of the harvest. "I couldn't mow around the trees the branches were hanging so low to the ground with apples." His daughter-in-law says he's not fooling. Same for the peach tree. It had produced fruit before, but not in the abundance of last year after Jones spiked a nail—it has to be a rusty one—beside it.

The old-timer isn't completely cut off from modernity. He has yet to grace the golden arches, but he went with Pam Jones the other day to Burger King. He was disappointed that they don't put chili and slaw on their hamburgers, as they do at JT's Diner in Liberty, a locally owned place that Jones frequents.

Jones is proud of being self-sufficient and believes that his life has been full and rich. "I don't think I've missed a thing," he says. The only skill he wishes he had is fiddling with cars and trucks. He depends on his son, David, for that. David recently replaced the motor in his dad's truck.

What worries his son and daughter-in-law is how much longer Preston Jones's own motor will last. They are grateful, though, that he has defied the prediction of being bedridden by now. He gets up, enjoys the day and makes plans for the future. His fishing pole, bait and tackle are in his truck. "I'm looking forward," he says, "to warm weather and going fishing."

Originally published in 2001.

Author's note: Preston Jones died in 2002 at age eighty-four.

ARCHITECT OF THE WHITE HOUSE LEARNED HIS CRAFT HERE

Many people know of the Truman Balcony at the White House but not of architect Lorenzo Winslow. He designed the balcony in 1947, and from 1948 to 1952 he gutted and rebuilt the home of presidents. The White House was nearing collapse from wear. A leg of Margaret Truman's piano broke through a decayed floor.

Greensboro residents can take a look at his handiwork at "The White House Meets the Bulldozer," a traveling exhibit from the White House Historical Association, on display through April 22 at the Greensboro Public Library gallery. The exhibit covers the Truman restoration.

The library exhibit's thirty-eight photos—shot during the restoration by photographer Abbie Rowe—show the White House reduced to bare exterior walls. One interior shot is of a bulldozer and dump truck inside among mounds of dirt where Thomas Jefferson, Abe Lincoln, Woodrow Wilson and Franklin Delano Roosevelt had lived.

The exhibit has local significance. Before becoming the architect of the White House, Winslow worked here as a draftsman and architect from 1920 to 1931, after pre–World War I work as a draftsman in Boston. His local legacies include the still-admired Tudor-style Irving Park Manor on North Elm Street and the Spanish colonial Winburn Court apartments on Tate Street.

A New England native, Winslow came here in 1921 as a draftsman for Greensboro architect Harry Barton after meeting Barton in Pinehurst. Barton had already designed the county courthouse on West Market Street and had many projects ahead at Woman's College, now the University of North Carolina at Greensboro, including Aycock Auditorium.

Winslow left Barton after two years to become a draftsman for another local architect, Raleigh James Hughes, who earlier had designed the Southeastern Building at Elm and Market Streets. In 1924, Winslow joined developer A.K. Moore, whose projects included the still beautiful Westerwood and Sunset Hills neighborhoods.

By 1927, Winslow was a full-fledged architect. He left Moore to set up a practice, first in the Piedmont Building and then the Southeastern. Besides Winburn Court and Irving Park Manor, Winslow designed a large Tudor house at 1705 West Market Street. He also designed a Universalist church, apparently never built. Benjamin Briggs, executive director of Preservation Greensboro, Inc., says that two mansions formerly owned by textile partners J.H. Adams and J. Henry Millis on High Point's North Main Street are attributed to Winslow.

Little is known of Winslow's personal life in Greensboro, except that he moved from Mendenhall Street to Park Avenue to Wharton Street to West Market and back to Wharton, to a lavender-colored bungalow still there. He arrived with a wife named Albinia and left with one named Garnette. He was said to be a skirt chaser, which may have cost him his White House position in the 1950s.

When the Great Depression pretty much ended architectural work in Greensboro, Winslow moved to Washington in 1931 to work for the government on public buildings and places. For a time, his boss was U.S. Grant III, the second big-name general for whom he worked. A decorated World War I veteran, Winslow served under General John J. "Blackjack" Pershing.

In Washington, Winslow helped design entrances to Arlington Memorial Bridge and prepared roads in Rock Creek.

According to an interview Briggs had last year with the architect's daughter, Vaughan W. Elliott of Georgetown, Winslow gained White House entry by winning a competition to build a pool where Franklin Roosevelt could exercise his polio-stricken legs. The small auditorium used by the White House press corps now covers the pool. "He emerged from that project as a favorite of the president and soon became the White House 'fixer,'" wrote William Bushong, historian for the White House Historical Association, in an article about Winslow for the White House Historical Association.

The president took a fancy to the corncob pipe–smoking, tweed suit–wearing Winslow, who claimed connections to New England aristocracy. The architect flattered Roosevelt and later Truman by submitting drawings to them for suggestions and approval. In 1940, FDR created the post of architect of the White House for Winslow, who also designed for the president the East Wing and a cozy library with a fireplace in former servant quarters. Bushong said in a telephone interview that Winslow was courtly "and was a somewhat bookish architect. He respected the past and wanted to preserve it, although he didn't always get his way."

It's not known if Winslow visited Greensboro again, but he maintained contact with his old boss, A.K. Moore. In 1933, according to Bushong's article, Winslow showed Moore a personal note from Roosevelt. It complimented Winslow on "the excellent taste you have exhibited in your selection of colors" for the swimming pool room.

After Roosevelt died, his successor, Truman, retained Winslow. The two caused a public furor when they built the Truman balcony to replace an awning-covered portico that Truman disliked. The news media and Congress howled: how dare Truman and Winslow tamper with the White House's historical integrity?

Later, a study showed that the White House was so wobbly that it faced collapse. Congress approved $5.4 million for restoration and modernization. Plans called for reusing as many original interior materials as possible. The long, arduous project had money shortfalls. Winslow had to cut corners, sometimes using modern materials instead of original. Although the project was deemed a success, Winslow publicly expressed dismay, especially about the sacrifice of original materials.

Bushong writes that Winslow's carping apparently angered Truman. In 1952, Truman, in essence, fired Winslow by demoting him. In an interview, Bushong says that another factor motivated Truman. Winslow was having an affair with a secretary in the architect's office. Truman, a devoted husband, was appalled that Winslow would cheat on his wife, who was blind. Winslow left government to become what Bushong calls "a gentleman architect" in Georgetown, working on a few private commissions, including restorations of Georgetown Presbyterian Church and New York Avenue Presbyterian Church in Washington. He later divorced his wife and moved to Florida, where he died in 1976 in his mid-eighties.

He may have been a sinner, but he was an architectural saint. Bushong writes that, with the exception of James Hoban, who designed the White House in 1792, and Charles McKim, who did a redesign in 1902, few others "can claim more design influence on the White House than Lorenzo Simmons Winslow."

Originally published in 2007.

EVEN IN 1914,
PEOPLE DEEMED TERMINALLY ILL
GOT A SECOND OPINION

Jasper Moody did, and a good thing, too.

This past April, in a *News & Record* story about the 100th anniversary of the founding of old St. Leo's Hospital and its nursing school, one line mentioned that the famous Mayo brothers of the Mayo Clinic in Minnesota visited St. Leo's and performed an emergency operation on a man not given long to live. Who would have thought that the person Charlie and Will Mayo cut open that day would speak up ninety years later through a descendant?

The man on the operating table was Jasper Moody, whose great-granddaughter, Kate McIver, a former college English teacher in Texas, now lives in Greensboro. She teaches music, plays piano at two churches and works in a cashier's booth in the parking decks of Piedmont Triad International Airport, where in between cars she writes her memoirs. She has written about Jasper Moody's operation, based on an account written by her late father, Bruce McIver, a preacher and writer who lived in Texas.

Kate McIver writes that Jasper Moody, about fifty at the time, lived in the small Chatham County community of Bear Creek. "Jasper was a semi-literate and dirt-poor farmer who struggled to feed a wife and ten children along the banks of Tick Creek," she says. In the summer of 1914, she continues, "Jasper developed severe stomach pains that could not be alleviated with herbs, tonics or home remedies." A doctor was summoned to Tick Creek, south of Siler City (old U.S. 421 crosses the stream). The doctor detected a large internal mass. "The tumor was, in his determination, inoperable," McIver says. "The family was advised to make their patriarch as comfortable as possible and to prepare for his death."

She says that after the doctor departed, Moody's sons gathered around the corncrib and decided to get a second opinion "before they simply gave up and allowed Pa to die." They knew about St. Leo's Hospital, opened in Greensboro in 1906 by the Catholic Sisters of Charity and closed in 1954. Its beautiful red brick building, including a nursing school, stretched nearly a block along Summit Avenue between Bessemer Avenue and Sullivan Street, across from what is now Summit Shopping Center.

The Moody brothers put their dad in a wagon on a mattress and took him to Ore Hill, the nearest rail stop. There they waited for the Atlantic & Yadkin Railroad train to Greensboro. The boys placed their dad on the mattress in the aisle of the lone passenger car. When the Moodys arrived at St. Leo's, it happened that Charles and Will Mayo were there. Their father, W.W. Mayo, had started in the 1880s what would become the Mayo Clinic in Rochester, Minnesota. There, his sons became renowned surgeons. Just why the brothers were in Greensboro isn't clear, but graduates of St. Leo's—including Hazel Fields, class of '37, who until her recent death was one of the oldest living graduates—confirm that they were there. The graduates say that out-of-state doctors often visited the hospital, which was considered the best in the state for a time.

St. Leo's Hospital, where the Mayo brothers, part of the family that founded the Mayo Clinic, removed a tumor from Jasper Moody of Chatham County in 1914. *Courtesy of Greensboro Historical Museum.*

"Charles and Will Mayo determined they could help Pa," Kate McIver writes, "and they rather quickly had him in an operating theatre (with other doctors spectating)." Margaret Moser and other St. Leo's alums claim that this was the first gastrointestinal bypass surgery ever performed in the United States. The Mayos performed a second operation to actually remove the grapefruit-sized tumor, Kate McIver says.

"Jasper Moody returned to Tick Creek, whose soil he farmed for another twenty years until his death in 1934,"

St. Leo's Hospital. *Courtesy of Greensboro Historical Museum.*

his great-granddaughter says. Moody nearly outlived his surgeons, who both died in 1939.

The story doesn't end there. Apparently, some of the later-day members of the family assumed that not all in the clan knew of the 1914 operation and that they probably had never heard of the Mayo Clinic. McIver says that in the 1980s, her father called from Texas to Chatham County to tell his elderly mother—Jasper Moody's daughter—that he had chronic orthopedic and cardiac problems and was going to the Mayo Clinic in Minnesota. "As he dialed the Siler City number," Kate McIver says, "he wondered how he could possibly convey to his hard-of-hearing, and rather sheltered, mother the significance and prestige of this world-renowned institution."

"I'm sure you haven't heard of it," he told her. "It's called the Mayo Clinic."

"Son," McIver quotes her grandmother as saying, "I know all about that place! Those Mayo brothers saved your grandpa's life."

And Mayo doctors—who came after "the boys," as Kate McIver's grandmother called the Mayo brothers—may have saved Bruce McIver. He lived another fifteen or so years, dying in 2001.

Originally published in 2006.

SPORTS

BETTY JAMESON'S LIFE LANDED IN ROUGH AFTER A BRILLIANT PRO GOLF CAREER THAT HAD ITS HIGHEST MOMENT IN GREENSBORO

Betty Jameson's forgetfulness doesn't come from old age or because the event she's trying to recall wasn't special. It's just that the 1947 U.S. Women's Open golf tournament was so long ago.

No spectacular shot stands out in her mind. She knows that the course was Starmount Forest Country Club in Greensboro and remembers the women she competed against. She vaguely recalls a city filled with lovely people and shaded by large oaks, maples and pines, which appealed to the artist in her. She didn't see many trees growing up in west Texas.

One vivid memory of Greensboro, however, glows. She won the tournament.

Today, nearly a half century later, the law could force her out of the Florida house she has occupied for more than thirty years and creditors can make her sell her paintings and furniture. But they can't take away the fact that she's a U.S. Open champ, an honor that puts her with the likes of Jack Nicklaus, Arnold Palmer, Tiger Woods, Nancy Lopez and Patty Berg. Knowing that she was once the best in her sport is a source of strength in these hard times she faces.

Wearing a white dress on that final round, Jameson shot a course record 70—6 under Starmount's women's par of 76—and finished with a 72-hole total of 295. It was the first time a woman had ever shot below 300 in a four-round tournament.

On the six-hundred-yard seventh hole, a par six for women and one of the longest holes in North Carolina, Jameson convinced sexists in the gallery that women can play the game. She made an eagle four.

Now, at seventy-six, and a resident of Delray Beach, Jameson hardly enjoys the good life of a former Open champ. Jameson is so broke that she recently had to sell two of her beloved paintings for $700. Friends say she has been skimping on eating and has lost forty pounds from her five-foot, eight-inch frame.

Likening life to golf, she believes that she can play her way out of this mess—just as she did long ago when slumps sent her to the practice tee for hours to drive away golf's demons. "I just have faith in God," she says by phone from Florida. "I think of God as love. I know I'm being taken care of. It hasn't been shown yet. I won't be on the street."

If times were better, she would be spending this week as a spectator at the Women's U.S. Open at Pine Needles Country Club near Southern Pines. The tourney has returned to North Carolina for the first time since the '47 event in Greensboro.

Pine Needles owner Peggy Kirk Bell, an excellent player during her prime, invited Jameson to attend. She and Jameson played together that last round at Starmount. "It was a great win for Betty," Bell recalls. "I was pulling for her. I wasn't going to win. She was a wonderful golfer." Friends would have paid for Jameson's trip to Pine Needles, but she says that the court fight over the house, which she once shared with the late pro Mary Lena Faulk, will keep her in Florida. Besides, she frets, she would get in Peggy Bell's way. "I would not have added anything to the tournament. Peggy has so much on her mind."

In today's television era, golfers who win the women's and men's U.S. Open are set for life because of endorsements and huge first-place checks. They make thousands just to wear a brand name on a visor. Jameson's time in the winner's circle arrived too early. Her big win came in only the second Women's Open ever played. She had been runner-up to the great Patty Berg in the first.

In her more than ten years on the Ladies Professional Golf Association Tour, Jameson won plenty of tournaments but not much money. Purses were puny in those days. Her only endorsement was for Spalding golf clubs, and it didn't pay much. She retired from tournament golf thirty-five years ago and, with Mary Lena Faulk, briefly ran a women's apparel shop in Southern Pines. "We just failed, flatly," she says. They then moved to Delray Beach and became teaching pros.

Now, she's enduring a sad twilight of a glorious golfing career. *Sports Illustrated*, in a recent article about Jameson, reported that at one point she was down to forty dollars in cash. To make ends meet, she sold pieces of furniture or her own paintings. Painting is her passion. During her golf days, she visited art galleries in tournament cities. She paints what she calls abstract impressionism.

According to *Sports Illustrated*, her financial ruin started when Faulk died of cancer last year. Faulk had family money. She owned the house and paid the bills. She made a will years ago leaving her property and money to a niece and other family members. She never got around to updating it to include Jameson, the daughter of a Texas newspaperman. As a result, Jameson is left with nothing except a $246 monthly Social Security check. She still lives in Faulk's house, but a court will soon decide whether she can stay.

The LPGA helped Jameson this winter by sending her a check for $10,000. After all, Jameson was a charter member of the tour and was among the first four players—Babe Didrikson Zaharias, Patty Berg and Louise Suggs being the others—inducted into the LPGA Hall of Fame. Her friends are distressed about her situation and want to do more to help. "I'm very sad about this," Bell says. "I think there will be something done."

The Faulk heirs and Jameson differ on certain points. The heirs say that they offered to let Jameson stay for two years rent-free in the house. Jameson's attorney, Bill Layton, says that the Faulk family said that Jameson could stay up to eighteen months but during that time would have to be looking for new quarters. Jameson is seeking court relief under a Florida law related to "oral wills"—meaning that Jameson says Faulk intended to leave her the house and income from Faulk's investments but never got around to putting it in writing. "It's a tough case," Layton says. "I have told her that from the beginning…She's a fighter. She's tough. She knows we are in a bad spot."

Layton sees a possible life-or-death outcome for Jameson. "For her to move, that might kill her," he says. "When you've been somewhere all your life, and you are comfortable, your physical and mental health can be tied to the place. Her memories are in that house."

Jameson still thinks of herself as a golfer, though she can't remember the last time she played eighteen holes. It has been years. Earlier this winter, she attended an LPGA tourney in Daytona Beach and went to the practice range to help a young LPGA pro who was having trouble with bunker shots. Jameson stepped into the sand to show how it was done. "I moved the ball a foot each time," she says, laughing as she recalled her embarrassment. "And that used to be my best shot."

She talks often about hitting the ball in the "sweet spot"—a small part of the club face that, when it meets a golf ball, creates an awesome feeling. Golfers don't even have to look up. They know they've hit a fantastic shot. "I specialized in hitting the ball in the sweet spot, taking dead aim and being able to drill the ball where you were looking," Jameson says. "I could do that. I could hit the ball as straight as anything." A long way, too. Her drives averaged about 235 to 240 yards, good for a woman or a man in those days when clubs and balls were less sophisticated.

Jameson hasn't been back to Greensboro since her victory. Old photos show her hitting her tee shot on the par-three tenth hole and putting on the ninth green. Spectators surround the green. A big movie camera on a tripod beside the green films the biggest women's tournament of the year. Sportswriter Al Thomy, then working for what's now the *Greensboro News & Record*, was in Jameson's gallery. "I remember she turned around and said, 'Thank you for following me.' The women golfers were so gracious, not like Sam Snead and that bunch," says Thomy, who later worked for newspapers in Atlanta and Dallas before retiring to Greensboro.

Jameson had turned pro a year or so before, after a distinguished amateur career in which she won the U.S. women's amateur championship twice. She also painted, read poetry and wrote. During World War II, she worked briefly as a reporter for the San Antonio paper. The city editor was always tapping his pencil waiting for Jameson to finish her stories. "I didn't like the deadlines," she says. "They were deadly. I wasn't as clever setting the story down as I would have liked to have been."

After the war, she devoted herself full time to golf, either playing or teaching, with a brief failed stint as a merchant in Southern Pines. Life was good until Faulk's death. Jameson admits that she depended on Faulk and the two rarely thought about the future. "She footed most of the bills," she says.

If only Jameson had come along later, when prize money on the women's tour escalated—the winner at Pine Needles will take home more than $150,000, compared with Jameson's $1,200 at Starmount. "I don't think in those terms," she says. "I'm glad I played in the period I did. I met so many wonderful people." But if she were fifty years younger and playing today's women's tour, "I would make a heck of a lot of money," she says with the confidence of a champ. "I might even say a helluva lot. I would be dominating the field as much as I did in my day. That is the confidence I had in myself. I felt I was that good."

Especially good that hot June week forty-nine years ago at Starmount. "I was hitting it," she says, "in the sweet spot."

Originally published in 1996.

Author's note: Thanks to help from the LPGA, of which she was a founder, and others, Jameson was able to enjoy her final years living in dignity in Delray Beach. She died in early 2009 in Florida.

PLEASANT GARDEN BASEBALL TEAM, THREE-PEAT STATE CHAMPS OF LONG AGO, FINALLY GET RECOGNITION

S winging a piece of lumber as a slugger for the Pleasant Garden High School baseball team, Roger Smith took aim at the commercial lumberyard that started where the weedy grass in right field ended. If a ball reached the yard, a home run usually resulted. While the batter raced around the bases, the opposing team's right fielder zigzagged through the yard chasing the ball.

During his time at Pleasant Garden, Smith's teams won the Class C state championship (for schools with fewer than two hundred students) three straight years: 1939, 1940 and 1941. They didn't just win—they massacred opponents, especially the '41 squad. Using a 29-hit barrage, including a Smith homer, Pleasant Garden trounced Rock Springs of Lincoln County 22–0 in the state semifinal game. Then, in the championship game played in Chapel Hill, Pleasant Garden thrashed like wheat Clarkton of Bladen County 19–4. Smith again hit a home run.

"We had talent," says Smith, now eighty-five and a McLeansville resident. "The boys just played together. The coach, Paul Hockett, saw the talent and brought it out of us."

The sports lexicon lacked the word "three-peat" back then, but it defined the Gardeners, as they were called. The town of Pleasant Garden, a few miles south of Greensboro, surely would have had a big celebration after the team's third championship. But 1941 was a bad year for exuberance. A war loomed. Now—sixty-six years later—the team's accomplishments are getting recognition. At a ceremony on September 30, the Pleasant Garden

The 1941 Pleasant Garden High School baseball team after winning its third straight state championship. *Courtesy of Pleasant Garden Historical Society and* Greensboro News & Record.

Historical Society brought back five of the six survivors from the 1939–41 teams: Smith, Doyle Quate, James Kirkpatrick, Branson Marley and Emmett Tucker Jr.

More than 125 people crowded into the town firehouse, where plaques were presented to the five and to families of departed teammates. Phil Way, a society member, historian and retired State Highway Patrol dispatcher, recalled how the cocky Clarkton players were convinced in 1941 of beating a bunch of farm boys from Pleasant Garden. The score was more like football than baseball. "Those boys were ashamed to go back home because they had been beaten so badly," Way says of Clarkton's nine. He adds that Clarkton might have been irritated, too, because Pleasant Garden's success over three years had much to do with the play of four Dunham brothers: George, Edwin, Willard and Marcus. The Dunham family had moved from Clarkton a few years before.

Way and the historical society decided on a resolution honoring the team after Way kept hearing stories from old-timers. Each time he'd mention a good ballgame, an elderly person would pipe up and say, "You should have been around in 1939, 1940 and 1941." Way called the North Carolina High School Athletic Association. The association confirmed the three championships and said that the feat hadn't been duplicated. An association official said that the team probably would have won a fourth if not for World War II. Many players left school to join the military.

In 1962, Pleasant Garden, Alamance and Nathanael Greene High Schools consolidated to form Southeast Guilford High. Smith recalls that the lumberyard at the end of right field wasn't the only oddity about the team's home field. A fence in right field, belonging to the Methodist parsonage, stood so close to home plate that a ball hit over the fence was scored a double instead of a home run.

The field lacked team benches. Players sat on the ground. Each player solicited local businesses for money for a twenty-dollar uniform. In return, the back of the jersey bore the business's name. Smith remembers one year being a walking, running ad for Cheek's Mercantile, a general store. Players who couldn't find uniform sponsors played in overalls.

Talk about team spirit. "The first year, I played without a uniform," Smith says. "A player with a uniform came up to me and said, 'You're better than I am,' and gave me his."

The war was a tougher opponent than any school team. According to research by society member Jane Kimel, one player, W.A. Moser, was killed in Pacific fighting. Emmett Tucker Jr. became a prisoner of war. He pitched only one game in '41, and it was a no-hitter. (Roscoe Taylor pitched all the rest and often struck out as many as fifteen players.)

The society hopes that money eventually can be found for a permanent marker to the '39, '40 and '41 teams. Reminders are few. Most players are dead. Their ball field is occupied by a building that's part of Pleasant Garden Elementary School. The lumberyard is still in business but has moved.

Kimel, in an article about the teams, says that the Major Leagues have players in the Baseball Hall of Fame in Cooperstown, New York, "but Pleasant Garden boys from the teams of 1939, '40 and '41 are in the Hall of Fame in our hearts."

Originally published in 2007.

SLAMMIN' SAM RETURNS TO STARMOUNT FOREST, WHERE HE WON FIRST GREATER GREENSBORO OPEN SIXTY YEARS AGO

Word spread quickly that the famous hillbilly golfer with the trademark straw hat was stroking putts on the practice green at Starmount Forest Country Club. Club employees and members emerged to see a legend in action. Soon, a photographer came roaring up the hill from Holden Road. "When I go to hell," grumbled a grinning Sam Snead, "there'll be a [expletive] camera waiting."

Blush, blush. Slammin' Sammy forgot that Marge Burns, ten-time state women's amateur champ and Starmount member, was putting nearby. He apologized.

The seventy-three-year-old Burns, nodding toward the ninth green, told Snead, soon to turn eighty-six, "I was right over there having a picnic and watching you play in 1938." That was the first time what was then called the Greater Greensboro Open (GGO) was played. Snead won it. He accepted the $1,500 winning check from celebrity band leader Fred Waring.

The tournament's name has changed often, and Snead hasn't played in it since the late 1970s, but his image remains associated with the event. He's here this week as part of the festivities of what's now called the Greater Greensboro Chrysler Classic, which is celebrating its sixtieth anniversary. Starting this year, a new trophy will be presented to the annual winner, the Sam Snead Cup. Who else? Snead won the tournament a record eight times over a thirty-seven-year span.

His Starmount visit for some practice putting was unplanned, a last-minute idea of former mayor Carson Bain, Snead's hunting and fishing buddy for fifty years. The timing, though, was perfect.

Starmount was where Snead played the first two rounds of the first-ever Greater Greensboro Open and then won when the final two rounds were played at Sedgefield Country Club. Two rounds were held at each course the first few years, and then the two clubs alternated years as host until 1956, when Starmount was awarded all four rounds.

After Snead won his seventh GGO title in 1960, course owner Edward Benjamin banished the golfer from Starmount for life. Benjamin was livid because Snead, in pocketing the $2,800 first-place check, criticized the condition of the course. Then as now with the tournament, now called the Wyndham Championship, the sponsors struggled to draw golf's big names. Snead could always be counted on to be in Greensboro. He was a PGA Tour marquee player even in his fifties. Even at age sixty-seven, he shot his age in a PGA Tour tournament.

Rather than lose its big star, the sponsoring Greensboro Jaycees moved the tournament to Sedgefield, where it stayed until 1976, when it relocated to Forest Oaks Country Club. In 1965 at Sedgefield, Snead captured his final Greensboro title. He was fifty-two years and ten months old, and he remains the oldest person to win a tournament on the regular PGA Tour. (The tour is open to pros of all ages, but a separate tour for players fifty and over has been held for nearly twenty-five years.)

Snead won more tournaments on the tour—eighty-one—than anyone to date. Now he has a trophy bearing his name. "It's wonderful," he said of this latest honor. "You don't have too many of those."

The rumbling you heard as Snead and Bain practiced putting was coming from Ed Benjamin's grave. Four years after Benjamin's death in 1980, Starmount's members bought the club from the Benjamin family. One of the membership's first actions was to name the winding, climbing road from the club's entrance Sam Snead Drive. Snead was invited to stop by anytime. And he has, entertaining members with stories, such as the time he explained to baseball great Ted Williams the difference between baseball and golf. "In golf," Snead said, "we have to play our foul balls."

Originally published in 1998.

Author's note: Until his death in 2002 in his late eighties, Snead tried to return annually to Greensboro to present the Sam Snead Cup and the first prize: now $900,000, compared to the $1,500 he won seventy-one years ago.

A RETURN TO TOURNEY
SPARKS MEMORIES

Ask Bill Rendleman what he shot in the first round of that first Greater Greensboro Open in 1938 and his answer sounds like some clever lawyer twisting a negative into a positive. "I tied Nelson," the retired businessman (who has a law degree) said Thursday while watching, sixty years later, the first round of the same tournament—now called the Greater Greensboro Chrysler Classic and played at Forest Oaks Country Club.

Nelson is Byron Nelson, regarded today as one of the greatest golfers to ever tee it up. Rendleman is telling the truth. He and Nelson both shot eighty at Starmount Forest Country Club, where the first two rounds were played before moving to Sedgefield Country Club for the final two. To those who don't keep up with big-time golf, eighty is lousy. Tournament leaders usually shoot in the sixties; Thursday's first-round leader, Hal Sutton, shot sixty-five.

But Rendleman's eighty was more of an accomplishment than Nelson's. Lord Byron, as he came to be known, was already a well-established touring professional. Rendleman was an eighteen-year-old student at Catawba College. The day before the tournament, he was standing on Main Street of his hometown of Salisbury, golf bag on his shoulder and right thumb extended. "I hitchhiked to the tournament," he said.

When he got to Greensboro, he checked in at his grandmother's house in downtown Greensboro. The next morning, he climbed aboard a city bus, golf bag again over his shoulder, and got off at what's now West Market Street and Holden Road. He walked the rest of the way to the Starmount course. After paying the $5 entry fee and a $2.50 caddy fee, he teed off

This may be the first Greater Greensboro Open in 1938. The golfer on the right with his hand on his hip is Sam Snead, who won the first tournament and seven more after that. The tournament is one of the oldest on the PGA Tour and is Greensboro's only major league sports event. *Courtesy of Harry Blair.*

in a field of golfers that included seven former U.S. Open champions and winners of other major championships.

More than seven thousand spectators roamed Starmount that day. Rendleman was awed by the many people—and nervous that most of them would be watching him, at least on the first hole. He bogeyed that hole, and many more after that.

Thursday, Rendleman returned to the tournament, which has undergone several name and course changes through the years but is still sponsored by the same organization as in '38, the Greensboro Jaycees. Realizing that fewer and fewer of the pioneers from that first tournament remain, Jaycees president Kurmar Lakhavani made sure that Rendleman had a ticket and parking place. No hitchhiking and bus rides this time.

Instead of seven thousand people—one of the biggest crowds on the PGA Tour in '38—some twenty-five thousand or more show up on some days of the tournament. The $5,000 total purse the first year has inflated to $2.2 million in 1998. "It's grown beyond conception," says Rendleman, seated in the big white tent known as the nineteenth hole, directly behind his favorite viewing spot, the thirteenth hole. "It's because of the good work of the Jaycees and others. There is no other tournament like it."

In recent years, Rendleman has been reliving his golfing youth through a young tour pro, Lee Porter, who learned the game at Greensboro Country Club, where Rendleman is a member. Despite their age difference, the two are close friends and have played golf together.

Right after he turned pro, Porter needed a warm place to practice during the winter. Rendleman has a home and membership in a club near Tampa. He told Porter to come on down. "He gave me the royal treatment," Porter said as he unloaded his clubs in the parking lot at Forest Oaks Thursday before teeing off, with Rendleman in the gallery. "He has always been a big supporter. He's a student of the game."

Rendleman worships the game, though not to the point of losing touch with reality. Any thoughts that he could make a living playing on the golf tour, as Porter is doing now, disappeared after that spring and summer of sixty years ago. In addition to the Greensboro tournament, he played in five other tournaments and found that his putting was suspect. He lacked whatever magical ingredient it is that distinguishes good golfers from great ones.

He returned to Catawba College and later graduated from law school at UNC–Chapel Hill. After navy duty during World War II, Rendleman began a business career that brought him to Greensboro in 1965. Rendleman did well enough to retire at age fifty-six. He then returned to his love of golf. "For twenty-two years, I've done nothing but play senior tournaments," he says. He won the Greensboro Seniors Amateur tournament three times. In 1990, he served as president of the Southern Seniors Golf Association, which has 1,200 members in thirty-six states. "The opportunities that golf has given me have been tremendous," he says. "To me, golf means people, places and faces."

Rendleman spends most of his time now at homes in Florida and in Waynesville in the North Carolina mountains, but he's in and out of Greensboro. His son, insurance agent Bill Rendleman Jr., lives here. At seventy-eight, Bill Sr. averages three rounds of golf a week and can still shoot in the seventies. He has shot his age each year since turning sixty-eight. He has yet to do it this year, but he's not worried. His birthday isn't until November.

Back to that first Greensboro golf tournament. Rendleman wanted to better that first-round eighty the next day. But when one checks old newspapers for a listing of scores for the second round, Rendleman's is not to be found. "Well, I'll tell you why," he says, with a pained look. "On the twelfth hole at Starmount, I hit my second shot into the creek, and I couldn't get it out. I made about a nine on the hole. I didn't turn in my score card when I finished." He got a chewing out from the Salisbury Country Club pro who was spectating that day. He called Rendleman a quitter. After that, Rendleman never missed finishing a round no matter how lousy he played.

Sweet swinging Bill Rendleman played as a teenager against famous pros in the first Greensboro Open golf tournament in 1938. *Courtesy of Rendleman family.*

Rendleman would play in one more Greensboro Open, in 1946, while stationed in the navy in Charleston, South Carolina. His scores? Eh, he says he doesn't remember. A search of newspapers shows that he shot an eighty and eighty-one, not good enough to qualify for the final thirty-six holes.

Originally published in 1998.

Author's note: Rendleman died in 2009, just short of ninety. He was shooting his age well into his eighties and was a spectator at what's now called the Wyndham Championship until his final years.

TOM ALSTON MADE HISTORY
AS FIRST BLACK ST. LOUIS CARDINAL
AND THEN FELL FROM BIG LEAGUES

Tom Alston says that he's always amazed when someone discovers the bright spot in his troubled life.

The other day, a baseball trivia buff sent him a faded photograph and asked that he autograph it. The picture shows a young, rangy player in a baggy St. Louis Cardinals uniform. He's swinging a bat. Bleachers of old Sportsman Park, where the Cardinals played in those days, appear in the background. The player is Tom Alston. It was 1954, the year he became the first black person to play for the Cardinals.

The club and newspapers made a big production out of Alston joining the team. Cardinal owner Augustus Busch, the beer tycoon, rented a Hollywood, California hotel suite for the announcement. Sports reporters and guests were treated to Budweiser and caviar. "The only blacks in the room were me and the valet who served the beer," Alston recalls.

His baseball career ended four years later. His life since then has been a series of strikeouts: attempted suicide, ten years in a North Carolina mental hospital and twelve years of being without a job. Even when not confined to a hospital, he suffered episodes resulting in emergency trips to the Guilford County Mental Health Clinic. Today, at fifty-six, Alston remains powerful looking at six feet, five inches, 255 pounds. He lives with his sister in a gray and white shingled house on Bothwell Street, a hilly street that dead-ends near the former L. Richardson Hospital, founded in the 1920s for Greensboro's black population.

Alston wears jeans and spends most days stretched on the sofa in his small living room. When he occasionally goes out, it's either to the mental health clinic or downtown to the Woolworth's store—site of another civil rights first—for coffee and pie. A child's book on baseball in the house is his only reminder of the sport that gained him fleeting fame. A few years ago, youngsters on his block organized a team—the Bothwell Cardinals—and asked him to be the coach. "I wanted to but I just wasn't up to it," he says.

Tom Alston grew up in Goshen, a small black community outside Greensboro on old U.S. 220 South. As a teenager, he belted homemade baseballs off a sandlot behind New Goshen United Methodist Church. Years later, the church would be the site of one of Alston's saddest moments. He attended what in those days was the city's all-black high school, Dudley, which at the time didn't have a baseball team. After serving in the navy during World War II, Alston went on to graduate from Greensboro's North Carolina A&T State University, which did have a baseball team, and Alston was the star. Later, he became a slugger for the old Greensboro Red Birds, a black semipro team that traveled widely and sometimes played teams in the old black Major Leagues, such as the Homestead Grays of Pittsburgh.

In 1962, he signed a contract with a low-level minor league team in California. He arrived seven weeks into the season. Seven weeks later, he was the league's leader in batting average, home runs and runs batted in (RBIs). The next year, Alston rose to the San Diego Padres, now a Major League

The field behind New Goshen Church where Tom Alston learned to play baseball. The field was also the home field for a time of the Goshen Red Wings (which became the Greensboro Red Wings), a black touring semi-pro team for which Alston played. *Photo by Jim Schlosser.*

team but back then a minor league club one notch below big league level. He had a respectful .297 batting average, whacked 23 homers and collected 101 RBIs. He impressed Major League scouts who followed the Padres.

In the early 1950s, black players remained scarce in the Majors. Brooklyn Dodger Jackie Robinson had broken the color barrier in 1947, followed by such other players as Dodgers Roy Campanella and Don Newcombe and the great Willie Mays of the New York (now San Francisco) Giants. Because the St. Louis Cardinals counted a substantial number of southerners as fans, it remained all white—until the team paid San Diego $110,000 for Alston. His starting salary, however, was $7,000, standard pay for rookies in those days. At Cardinals spring training in Florida, the big first baseman played alongside famous white players he had read about in newspapers and seen in newsreels: Stan Musial, Red Schoendienst, fellow North Carolinian "Country" Slaughter, Harvey Haddix, Steve Bilko and Walker Cooper. "Really, it wasn't all that exciting," Alston says. "I wasn't awed by nobody."

Considering the era, when much of society was still segregated, Alston believes that he was treated fairly. The players, he says, weren't overly friendly but weren't rude. Still, until another black player joined the team later that season, Alston slept alone in train compartments and in hotels. He dined alone. When the Cardinals played spring training exhibition games in the South, Alston had to stay in shabby hotels for black people, separated from his white teammates. "Those were the days of segregation, and it was a way of life," he says matter-of-factly.

Alston didn't succeed with St. Louis. At about the halfway point in each of his four seasons, the team would ship him back to the minor leagues. There he would clout a bunch of homers—including a mammoth 420-foot blast in Omaha—and then be recalled in late season to the Cardinals. "Tom was great defensively, but he had trouble hitting breaking pitches," says Jim Toomey, the Cardinals' public relations director at the time, referring to pitchers throwing curveballs that the inability to hit ruined the careers of many big league prospects.

Alston's most glorious day in the Majors was a doubleheader against the Giants. Still, he got only a small piece of the glory. Teammate Stan Musial hit five home runs in the two games, while Alston and Wally Moon each hit one. The trio's photo appeared together the next day in newspapers across the nation.

Alston knows that he didn't live up to expectations with the Cardinals. His four-year Major League average was a meager .234 with four home runs. He says that he played never feeling fit physically or mentally. The first year he signed with the Cardinals, he says, he heard strange voices in his head. "I don't remember what they said," he says, "but it scared me to death." He was playing for a Mexican team before going to St. Louis at the time, and "I left Mexico feeling drained. I've never felt good since then." By his third year with the Cardinals, "I felt people were looking at me funny," he says. "I wondered what I was doing wrong." The voices returned at the end of that season. Rather than have him play off-season ball, the Cardinals sent Alston home to Greensboro to rest.

One night, he says, he heard a woman's voice screaming at him to "commit suicide, commit suicide." With a razor blade, he drove to a remote spot in the Goshen community and slashed his wrist. He inflicted only minor wounds. A sheriff's deputy happened by and took Alston home.

When the new season started, Alston's weight dropped from 197 to 175 pounds. The Cardinals became worried. They sent him to a hospital. Although he had never told team officials about the voices, a psychiatrist was sent to

examine him. "He didn't ask no questions or nothing," Alston recalls, "just administered shock treatment." Within a month, Alston felt better and was playing better. Still, the next season the Cardinals didn't invite Alston to return. His playing days were over.

He remained in Greensboro and had a brush with the law. He says that he can't remember what he did wrong, but he spent a month on a chain gang. Not long after that, he walked into Goshen Church, empty at the time, sprinkled kerosene and set the building on fire. The church was destroyed and a new one was built later. "I can't explain why I did it," he says. "It wasn't a voice or anything like that. It was impulse. I kept a prayer book for those years,

Tom Alston's grave behind the ball field in the Goshen community. *Photo by Jim Schlosser.*

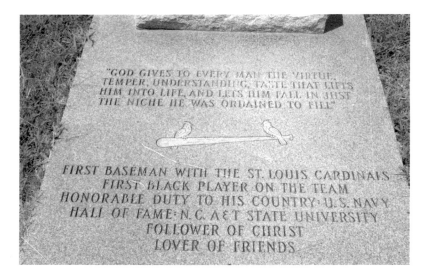

"GOD GIVES TO EVERY MAN THE VIRTUE,
TEMPER, UNDERSTANDING, TASTE THAT LIFTS
HIM INTO LIFE, AND LETS HIM FALL IN JUST
THE NICHE HE WAS ORDAINED TO FILL"

FIRST BASEMAN WITH THE ST. LOUIS CARDINALS
FIRST BLACK PLAYER ON THE TEAM
HONORABLE DUTY TO HIS COUNTRY: U.S. NAVY
HALL OF FAME: N.C. A&T STATE UNIVERSITY
FOLLOWER OF CHRIST
LOVER OF FRIENDS

Alston's grave. Note the St. Louis Cardinal symbol in the middle: two cardinals on a bat.
Photo by Jim Schlosser.

and in it I wrote that Goshen needed a new chapel." As a result of the fire, he spent the next eight years at a state mental institution in Goldsboro. Released in 1967, he returned to Greensboro. Two months later, he set fire to his apartment. He was sent back to a state mental institution.

He came back to Greensboro in 1969, and he says, "I have been doing pretty good since then. Take medication and go to the mental health clinic quarterly. I still hear voices." He'd like to be treated at a nationally known mental health center, but he lacks the money. He writes letters to former ballplayers asking for help. He gets nice letters in return, he says, but no money. He says that Willie Mays sent an autographed picture.

Still, not everyone has forgotten. His alma mater, A&T, inducted him into its Sports Hall of Fame in 1972. Because of their rarity, his baseball cards—bubble gum companies printed cards of all players during their time in the Majors—have become collector's items. The more obscure a player, it seems, the more valuable his card.

In 1977, he made a trip back to St. Louis for the first time in nearly twenty years. The team was on the road playing, but its trainer was at the team's new Busch Stadium, and he remembered Alston. "He took me into the locker room and gave me a rubdown, just like old times," Alston says. "We went out in the middle of the stadium and he pointed to the right field seats and said, 'Tom, do you think you could hit one out there?' I told him I thought I could."

He says, "What really surprises me is how people find out about me. I get letters occasionally, and I'll be walking through Woolworth's [site of the 1960 desegregation sit-ins] or someplace and someone will holler, 'Hey, Mr. St. Louis Cardinal.' It makes me feel kinda good."

Originally published in 1982.

Author's note: Tom Alston died in 1993 at sixty-seven.

CITY HAD GREEN BAY PACKERS
A WEEK A YEAR

M any think of the obvious at Thanksgiving: a dining room table filled with good food, family togetherness and gratefulness for the blessings Americans enjoy. Greensboro's old-timers remember another former symbol of the day: the Green Bay Packers. From 1951 to 1963, the Packers played the Detroit Lions on TV every Turkey Day in Detroit, usually in snow or mud. Detroit still plays that day, indoors, but not against the Packers.

From 1955 to 1959, Green Bay was Greensboro's team. In early September, the Packers flew into the city, checked into the Oaks Motel on Summit Avenue and spent a week training for an exhibition against the Washington Redskins, the South's only pro team at the time.

The Redskins trained for a week in Winston-Salem for the Packer game, which was played in the Twin City's still standing Bowman Gray Stadium. Green Bay practiced near its motel at War Memorial Stadium. When the stadium wasn't available, the team went six miles to the west to Guilford College's field.

During one Packer workout, Guilford president Clyde Milner, a scholarly man who knew nothing of football, happened by the field. He marveled at the size, speed and strength of the men running about the field. A famous story was born. In a *News & Record* story written years later by former staff writer Wilt Browning, former Guilford football coach Herb Appenzeller recalled, "Dr. Milner walked up behind me and stood quietly watching what was going on for a few minutes. Then, just before he walked away, he said, 'Oh, my good man, I believe we're going to have a pretty good ball club this year.'" Milner thought that the likes of Bart Starr, Max McGee, Fred

Thurston, Emlen Tunnell, Paul Hornung and Jerry Kramer were newly enrolled Guilford students.

The Packers enjoyed first-class quarters at the Oaks, which in the 1950s offered color TVs in rooms. Each day, the Packers walked a block to Summit Shopping Center to fuel up their stomachs at the Glass House Restaurant. Locals gasped as they watched the team practice. Most had seen pros only on TV. In person, they looked so much stronger and bigger than college players. Their punters boomed the pigskin farther than any college player. The Packers' placekicker, Paul Hornung, also the star running back, split uprights from distances that college teams wouldn't dare kick from back then. While college teams tended to run far more than they passed, pro teams threw often and long. The Packers looked old, too. Some had bald heads. Tunnell, who had been traded from the New York Giants to the Packers, had by 1959 been playing pro ball since 1948.

That last year the Packers were in Greensboro, they had a new coach, Vince Lombardi. He's now a legend for his fierce temper and determination to win. Nevertheless, one local sportswriter described him as "personable." A just chewed-out player would have laughed. Lombardi cut no player, no matter how good, any slack. He said that the reason Paul Hornung, who had been a great quarterback at Notre Dame, wasn't playing that position for the Packers was because Hornung was a lousy passer.

The coach was so strict on these grown men that he wouldn't let them swim in the Oaks pool, according to Arthur Daley, a retired Green Bay, Wisconsin sportswriter, interviewed in 1996 by the *News & Record* when the Carolina Panthers (who weren't born until the 1990s) played the Packers in Green Bay. Daley said that Lombardi thought swimming was bad for football muscles.

The Packers and Washington exhibition game was called the Piedmont Bowl. The Packers had lost to the Skins in the previous games. In fact, during the 1958 season, Green Bay won one regular season game. Then came Lombardi. The Packers beat the Redskins in the '59 game 20–13. Hornung scored all the Packers' points, including kicking a forty-six-yard field goal.

For Green Bay, a golden era began that year in Greensboro. NFL titles and Super Bowl victories lay ahead under Lombardi. To put it in Thanksgiving terms, it was in Greensboro that Lombardi began making thoroughbreds out of players who before had played like turkeys.

Originally published in 2006.

CONCOCTIONS

WHY APINOL VANISHED FROM CITY'S MEDICINE CHEST

Surely, Greensboro officials begged her to change her mind. Surely, the county or city offered tax incentives to stay.

In fact, no one pleaded for her to keep Apinol in Greensboro, where it had been since 1967 after relocating from Wilmington, where it was founded in 1903. It took only a modest-sized truck for owner Cindy Simmons to move the Apinol Corp. from Greensboro to a town near Birmingham, Alabama, in August 2003, during the company's centennial year.

Apinol's departure is only now being recognized because Simmons called the *News & Record* recently to say that the company's one and only product, Apinol, is still healing people across the country and has a pedigree history. The product was the idea of Hugh McRae, who belonged to one of Wilmington's most prominent families. Hugh McRae Park is one of the places named for him in the Port City. He also owned Grandfather Mountain in western North Carolina and willed it to his grandson, the famed photographer Hugh Morton.

Hugh Morton, who says he was raised on Apinol, says, "If you've ever used it, you're a believer."

Founder McRae boasted that Apinol soothed and healed paper cuts and other lacerations, insect and chigger bites, chapped lips, sunburn and other types of burns. It relieved pains in the joints. It would cure, he said, whatever ailed Fido the dog, Chessie the cat or, in rural areas, the livestock in the barnyards.

The McRaes warned people not to take Apinol internally, but some people did. One favorite method was to coat Apinol on chewing gum to make toothaches disappear.

Through the years under different owners, the company accumulated file folders of unsolicited testimonials. A nurse in Charlotte wrote, "I raised my children on Apinol. It is the most soothing and effective antiseptic I've ever used. In fact, it is all I ever use." A former owner of Apinol, Warren Bass of Greensboro promises, "It will cure everything except heartache." Bass bought the company from a neighbor, Ted Whitson, who in turn bought it from Hugh McRae II, another grandson of the founder. Judy Morton of Greensboro, Hugh Morton's daughter, says that she can still hear her grandmother shouting, "Put some Apinol on it," each time she had a nick or an itch.

The McRaes still speak those words when medical emergencies arise. Hugh McRae II of Wilmington says that he stepped the wrong way into a golf course bunker on a recent Sunday and pulled a muscle in his left calf. "I rubbed Apinol on it two or three times Sunday night and the pain was gone Monday morning," he says.

McRae says that the family started making Apinol to increase the revenues of the family enterprises, which in 1903 included coastal farms and nurseries and land development at Wrightsville Beach and Grandfather Mountain in the western part of the state. The family chose a simple practical name for the concoction. Apinol is an abbreviation of sorts for "a pine oil" product. Hugh McRae II says that in southeastern North Carolina, where the woods are full of loblolly and longleaf pines, the benefits of rubbing pine oil on whatever hurt had been well known since early days.

The McRaes marketed Apinol in North and South Carolina and Virginia. For a while, the company produced Apinol Soap, aimed at mechanics who found regular suds not tough enough to remove oil and grease stains. As people moved from the Carolinas and Virginia, they took Apinol with them and introduced it to neighbors, who ordered bottles from the McRaes.

Hugh McRae II says that the Boston Red Sox used it to ease sore muscles during spring training. "It was a nice money maker," he says of the product.

And overhead was low. A Wilmington woman who worked for the McRaes watched over the making and marketing of Apinol. Subsequent owners also ran it as a one- or two-person operation. At one point, the McRaes considered mass producing Apinol in concert with the Richardson family of Greensboro, who owned Vicks Chemical Company, makers of Vicks VapoRub and Vicks Cough Drops. But the Depression killed that idea.

Concoctions

In a weak moment in the 1960s, Hugh McRae II says, he sold Apinol to Ted Whitson of Greensboro. Using Hercules Pine Oil, Whitson made Apinol in a building on Patterson Street near the Greensboro Coliseum. Whitson sold the company to Warren Bass, who was assisted by John Bates of Greensboro. Bates eventually bought the company.

Simmons says that she contacted Bates two years ago to buy a case of Apinol because she couldn't find any in Alabama. When Bates expressed an interest in selling the company, a deal was struck. She grew up on Apinol in Roanoke, Virginia, where her father, a mechanic with Norfolk & Western Railroad, had long used the product for cuts and aches suffered on the job. Her father later left the railroad and moved to Alabama, where he founded a business that rebuilds turbochargers and fuel pumps. Simmons now runs that business, as well as Apinol.

"If I put the time into it, it would be better," she says of Apinol's sales. She doesn't release figures but says that Apinol makes money. She hopes to make more. She plans to advertise the product and be more aggressive with marketing. Now, she relies on repeat mail-order business. Some independent drugstores, including those that belong to the North Carolina Mutual Drug Consortium, carry Apinol. The Eckerd (Rite-Aid) chain used to stock Apinol. But previous owners Bass and Bates say that chains don't like products such as Apinol because a bottle lasts an eternity. Bates gets his from Burton's, an independent pharmacy on Lindsay Street downtown.

The McRae family still does its part to spread the word about Apinol. On a trip to England, Hugh McRae II presented a bottle to a woman in Britain's aristocracy. "She now swears by it," he says. "She sent me a letter recently and asked if I would please send her another bottle."

Originally published in 2005.

AH, THE SWEET SMELL
OF AN EL MORO

The city's bicentennial celebration calls for firing up a cigar, a good old Greensboro-made stogie. Ideally, the cigar of choice would be a General Greene, named for the Revolutionary War general for whom the city is named. The Greene brand was made here early in the twentieth century by hotel owner W.F. Clegg. He had a cigar plant on South Elm Street near his hotel, the Clegg, which hugged the Southern Railway train depot where fifty passenger trains stopped daily.

The Greensboro Historical Museum's "Welcome to the Gate City" exhibit includes displays of a General Greene cigar box on the counter of the reproduced Clegg Hotel lobby. Jon Zachman, a curator, says that the box contains no General Greenes. Two other display boxes include real examples of one of the city's best-known and widely sold brands, El-Rees-So. John Rees, a former Southern Railroad employee, started making El-Rees-So about 1915. His plant was on the second floor over a first-floor cigar shop he and his wife owned at Elm and Sycamore (now February One Place).

In 1926, Rees joined with other investors to form the El Moro Cigar Co., which made El Moros and El-Rees-So at a plant at South Elm and Lee Streets. When the tornado of 1936 snuffed out the plant, El Moro built a bigger factory at the northeast corner of Greene and McGee Streets.

Greensboro was the state's—indeed the region's—cigar capital for most of the first half of the twentieth century. Officially, about seven cigar factories operated at one time, but old city directories from about 1918 to the late

EL-REES-SO CIGARS

Mild, Fragrant Quality

Why have EL-REES-SO sales doubled and thribbled since we began business? There must be a reason.

Began business August, 1913. Manufactured during balance of year	90,000	Cigars
Manufactured during 1914	675,000	"
Manufactured during 1915	2,250,000	"
Manufactured during 1916	7,325,000	"
Manufactured during 1917 (approximately)	15,000,000	"

Expect to manufacture approximately 20,000,000 during 1918.

EL-REES-SO CIGAR COMPANY
MANUFACTURERS

An advertisement for El-Rees-So Cigars, one of the many cigar brands made in Greensboro from the late nineteenth to mid-twentieth century. *Courtesy of Greensboro Historical Museum.*

1930s indicate that as many as fourteen companies rolled out cigars during that period. Another company made boxes for cigars. A 1922 story in the *Greensboro Daily News* reported, "Every time the clock runs around 24 hours in Greensboro the factories in the city can point to nearly 300,000 new cigars." That amounted to 30 million cigars annually.

Local historian Gayle Fripp, in her book, *Greensboro: A Chosen Center, an Illustrated History*, published in 1980, wrote that Greensboro's cigar factories could "turn out more cigars than those in any city between Baltimore and Tampa."

The El-Rees-So Co. grew rapidly, employing three hundred people by 1917, big for a city of ten to fifteen thousand. An ad pamphlet for the company boasted that "all the cigars are made by girls...pretty girls."

Another manufacturer, Seidenberg & Co., operated a five-story factory at Gaston (now West Friendly Avenue) and Greene Streets. A 1911 promotional article said that the Greensboro plant employed 260 people, nearly all women, who were paid thirty-five to forty dollars a week. They produced such brands as the Little Tam, the Little Zoz, the Little Tiberius, the Class and the Lady Churchill.

A drawing of El Moro Cigar plant, probably about 1927, when it opened in the southern end of downtown following a merger between the El Moro and El-Rees-So brands. *Courtesy of Greensboro Historical Museum.*

Naturally, Greensboro gentlemen (women were not supposed to smoke cigars) puffed this economic booster for the city. Smoke shops stood throughout the downtown, filled with cigars in boxes that manufacturers took pride in elaborately decorating. These stores became gossip shops. The Tuxedo Cigar Store, 104 South Elm Street, advertised that within its walls "businessmen, policemen, office holders, lawyers and the 'intellectual classes' gathered to buy cigars and latest periodicals and 'get a line on who's who in Greensboro.'"

Oddly, the first cigars associated with Greensboro came from a family whose name today is equated with textiles, the Cones, who founded Cone Mills, once one of the nation's largest cotton and denim producers. In 1890, before going into the yarn business, brothers Moses and Ceasar Cone, and their father, Herman, owned a large wholesale grocery business in Baltimore. As the brothers traveled the South, they handed out to grocery store owners fine boxes of Cone Cigars, probably made in Baltimore, where the Cones then lived. The Greensboro museum has a box of Cone cigars on display.

Residents knew that Greensboro was a cigar town not just from the sweet aroma that saturated downtown. Farmers in horse-drawn wagons piled high with harvested leaves crowded downtown streets. W.F. Clegg provided livery services for the horses and allowed farmers to sleep on his factory floor.

The cigar industry arose fast and burned out almost as quickly. By the mid-1950s, the public regarded cigars as outdated. They had lost out to cigarettes, which had become hot or cool, depending on your choice of words. Perhaps World War II won the day for cigarettes. Manufacturers gave away millions of cigarettes to military people and continued to do so for years afterward.

In 1955, Greensboro's last cigar company, El Moro, closed, after being purchased by the T.E. Brooks Co. of Red Lion, Pennsylvania. The company continued to make El-Rees-So and El Moro brands, but in Red Lion. The company deemed the Greensboro plant too outdated. It was demolished in 1956. The site, at the corner of McGee and South Greene Streets, is now a parking lot.

Older Greensboro residents remember El Moro being made here. Wouldn't it be delightful if a big batch could be made to hand out in all those fancy new restaurants on South Elm Street? They stand in what used to be the smell zone for those cigar factories.

Originally published in 2008.

Author's note: Greensboro may have burned out as a cigar maker, but it is now the world headquarters for Lorillard Co., the maker of such cigarette brands as Newport and Kent.

A SAUCE THAT TASTES GOOD
AND IN A BOTTLE THAT WILL MAKE
YOU BLUSH

It took a lawsuit, but the sauce with the side-splitting label has returned to where Martha Boren says it belongs. "I figured it ought be in the Boren family because that's where it started," says Boren, who at seventy-three has gone to great trouble and expense to become the latest in a line of Borens to produce Samson's Sauce. It's a meat sauce that enjoys a cult following. Until earlier this year, it was available for decades in some grocery stores and restaurants and soon will be again, Boren says. She says some Harris Teeter stores already have it.

Martha Boren's father-in-law, Gurney Simpson Boren Jr., concocted the sauce in 1925 in his attic. He stirred it in a barrel with a canoe paddle. Boren, who loved to cook and whose nickname was Samson, put that name on the label. He filled empty soda and whiskey bottles with sauce, slapped on the label and gave them to friends. He didn't do it for money. He was a vice-president in the family-owned Pomona Terra Cotta Co. (Another branch of Borens founded Boren Brick, now Hanson Brick.)

In the 1940s, Boren designed a new label boasting that the sauce had powers beyond enhancing steaks, stews, seafood and other foods. He inserted a French word meaning "the rest is just foolishness." That was followed by claims that the sauce was good for baldness, hangover and amnesia and as an aphrodisiac. "Twenty drops will cure insanity or else drive you crazy. Not recommended for prickly heat, poison ivy, shortness of breath or hemorrhoids."

When Boren died in 1954, his sons, Gurney Boren III and Maxwell Boren, continued the sauce. They added ingredients and expanded distribution.

Maxwell soon died, and another brother, Jimmy Boren, Martha's husband, joined Gurney Boren in making the sauce. When Jimmy became ill, Gurney Boren was on his own.

By then, Harris Teeter, the Fresh Market and many restaurants stocked Samson's Sauce. For years, it also graced the tables of the Greensboro Country Club, where Gurney Boren was a member. Sauce deliveries weren't always predictable because of Gurney Boren's work ethic. He spent hours at the country club playing gin rummy. When he needed money, he would retreat to a cinder block building behind his house on Parrish Street to make sauce.

Later, to expand production from two hundred cases a year to one thousand, he leased a warehouse. Government inspectors visited and didn't find the product's label amusing. "Uncle Sam just doesn't have a sense of humor," Boren said in a 1988 interview. "They're just trying to protect one incompetent idiot out of a million who might pour a bottle over his head." Boren had to make a new, humorless label for bottles distributed to food stores and restaurants. For friends and others who ordered from him personally, he kept the humorous label.

In the late 1990s, Gurney Boren left the sauce making in the hands of a helper. He took off for Las Vegas to test a system he had dreamed up to win at cards. When he returned—broke—after nearly three years, he found himself without a business. The helper claimed ownership, citing a law pertaining to "abandoned businesses."

Crushed, Boren returned to Vegas, where he died in 2004 in his seventies. He willed the copyright to Samson's Sauce to Jimmy and Martha Boren. Jimmy Boren, who remains ill and unable to help make the sauce, passed the recipe to his wife. Just in case, Gurney Boren had left a copy of it in a safe-deposit box, along with recipes for other sauces he had hoped to make someday.

Gurney Boren's former helper wasn't about to give up the business. Martha Boren went to court last March and, through mediation, regained control of Samson's Sauce. She's now getting the sauce back on the market, plus selling it over the Internet. A website is being prepared. The former helper had sold a lot of sauce over the telephone. Martha Boren went to lots of trouble to get the telephone number on the label transferred to her cellphone. As a result, she gets calls every day from as far away as California. "I had a man call from Dakota, Texas, the other day," she says. "I didn't know there was a Dakota, Texas."

The product has spread across the country through word of mouth and by Greensboro people who moved and took bottles with them. Also, local companies bought caseloads, stamped their names on the labels and gave bottles to customers in far-flung places. She believes that Gurney Boren III would be tickled to know she is making the sauce. It's a shame, she says, that he didn't push the product harder. "He could," she says, "have made a good living."

Originally published on October 4, 2006.

CONSTRUCTION UNEARTHS OLD VICKS MEDICINE BOTTLES AT FORMER FACTORY SITE

B ritt Preyer hit pay dirt.

Hands and clothes filthy, Preyer returned home the other day with boxes of bottles filled with family heirlooms—ancient bottles of Vicks VapoRub and other products made by Vicks Chemical Co. His great-grandfather, Lunsford Richardson, invented Vicks VapoRub in the 1890s in eastern North Carolina. Lunsford perfected and named it in a downtown Greensboro drugstore that he bought in 1898. The product's name honored his brother-in-law, Dr. Joshua Vick.

Preyer had gotten a call from a relative about land being cleared for apartments on Milton Street, off Spring Garden Street. Earth-moving machinery had unearthed thousands of old medical bottles. Vicks Chemical's main plant had stood on the site from 1910 until it was demolished in the mid-1960s. "They were just dumped there," Preyer says of the bottles. "Maybe it was a sample overrun. It's hard to know." Digging with a garden trowel, in two and a half hours Preyer unearthed several hundred bottles of various colors and sizes. He returned the next day and took home several hundred more. Some still contained VapoRub.

Preyer already had some old Vicks bottles that he had bought at antique shops. He thought he knew the size and shape of all company bottles, "but some of these I have never seen before." The most numerous are tiny, spherical and royal blue with "Vicks" on one side and "Drops" on the other. These bottles and others probably date to the early twentieth century. A construction worker found among them a Coca-Cola bottle with a 1915 date.

Bottles of Vicks VapoRub and other Vicks products strewn about the ground after construction began in 2008 on a new apartment complex on Milton Street. *Photo by Jim Schlosser.*

Bottles boxed by Britt Preyer, great-grandson of VapoRub inventor Lunsford Richardson. Preyer spent hours digging for bottles at the old plant site. *Photo by Jim Schlosser.*

Concoctions

Historian Gayle Fripp, in her book *Greensboro: A Chosen Center*, wrote that Vicks Chemical increased VapoRub sales "through the distribution of free samples and five million jars were sent to potential customers in 1917." Vicks products were in high demand during the Spanish flu pandemic of 1918–19.

Born in 1951, Preyer says that he never saw the Vicks plant on Milton, but he does recall a second plant, built in 1936, at Cridland Drive and Wendover Avenue, across from Latham Park. That operation made cough drops. The sweet scent of menthol and camphor wafted through the neighborhood.

The Milton Street plant was demolished after Vicks Chemical—by then known as Richardson-Vicks—built a big new plant on West Market Street in the mid-1960s. Procter & Gamble now owns the company and continues making VapoRub and other Vicks products.

The Milton Street plant may be long gone, but not the aroma. "Sometimes," says Chris Staley, construction foreman at the apartment site, "you can get a whiff of the Vicks."

Preyer plans to give bottles to family members at the next family reunion and will offer some to the Greensboro Historical Museum. The tiny bottles have added sentimental value to him. His grandfather, W.Y. Preyer—who married Lunsford Richardson's daughter, Mary Norris Richardson—started as a traveling Vicks salesman. He handed out samples like those his grandson dug up.

It took the worldwide Spanish flu epidemics to make VapoRub a staple in medicine chests. In the 1920 outbreak, demand for VapoRub in Greensboro was so great that the product had to be rationed, according to Fripp.

Preyer believes that the VapoRub in the old bottles remains potent. He has a bottle that he estimates to be at least fifty years old that he bought at an antique shop. When he feels an ailment coming on, he reaches for the bottle on his office shelf and rubs in VapoRub. Does it still have punch? "Absolutely," he says.

Originally published in 2008.